MW01404712

UNREST

UNREST

EXPERIENCING THE POWER OF SABBATH

Tim Ingram

UNREST

Experiencing the Power of Sabbath

illuminate CHURCH
Celebration, Florida
www.illuminatechurch.com

1st Edition

ISBN: 978-1-947153-54-7

Cover Design Bruno Arnese
Interior Layout Rachel Newhouse

To Jesus. Still my first love. Look at what You have done. I am grateful. And to TACOE. What a ride, huh? I love you a silly amount.

CONTENTS

INTRODUCTION

As an introduction, allow me to introduce that I have no idea how to write an introduction. No training. No schooling. Just writing here what I think might be helpful perspective as you dive into what I believe the Lord asked me to share in this book. I suppose, then, an introduction introduces you to the material by allowing the reader to see into my brain and heart as I wrote what you are about to read (or maybe not read after this introduction...oh, and it's at this point I should mention I am an external processor.)

I went to Asbury Theological Seminary which has its main campus in Wilmore, Kentucky, however I attended all my classes at the extension campus in Orlando, Florida as it was significantly closer to home. My very first class was with a legend (at least to me) of a professor, Dr. Robert Tuttle. If you picture an extremely brilliant professor with a never-ending source of energy, a piercing gaze with incredible passion for the subject material, you might picture Dr. Tuttle. As a new seminary student, I found him daunting. Him smart. Me not smart. With great trepidation, I turned in my first paper. In high school and at the University of Florida, I had been primarily an A student. Grades came easily most of the time. I had hoped that trend would continue in this new venture. The paper came back, the grade on the final page.

C+.

Really?

Upon seeing the grade in ink on the last page, I went flush with emotions ranging from, "I am the dumbest person in seminary on the planet," to, "Dr. Tuttle is the dumbest professor on the planet," to, "Clearly God is trying to tell me to quit ministry." Quite the optimist, aren't I? There was one comment under the grade that cleared everything up immediately. Written there in Dr. Tuttle's own hand, "Great content, but too much like you are having a conversation and not an academic paper. Clean it up." Very Tuttle-like. He wasn't wrong. I write like I speak. There was a choice for me to make. I made up my mind that I wasn't called to be an academic, but a pastor. Nothing wrong with either one, but certainly distinct endeavors, at least for me. I decided I was going to write conversationally, with intent on the reader understanding the content, and the scene, and the feeling, and the color of the canvas. I still write conversationally. I preach conversationally. As a result, this book will therefore take on a more casual nature. No footnotes or diagrams, none of the seemingly prerequisite trappings that give a book its authoritative place in the annals of higher education. It's just not who I am. I can't deliver a book in a form disingenuous to who I've been all these years. "Wow, suddenly Tim sounds like Dr. Ingram!" Nope. I am who I am, by God's grace, and that is what you will encounter as you read. If you are the more academic type, welcome! You will find within these pages some recommendations of books that will fill the gaps in for you nicely.

Also of note, the content of this book was written over five years before it was printed. As you will read, my life went through a tailspin seemingly out of nowhere. My journey to recovering stability and joy in my life is the basis of this book, which was first a message series I delivered to our church, illuminate church (not capitalized on purpose). The Elders believed it was necessary teaching for the greater Body of Christ and encouraged me to transfer the message to book form. Which happened quickly. The message series became a rough draft of a book...but then...I went to a conference.

There, someone else, someone who had already sold millions and millions of books, walked out on platform and announced, "I've written a new book!' Great. I love this man's books. Perhaps I'll purchase a copy before I leave the conference, depending on the subject. Take one guess. Exact same subject as the book I had just written. Phhhhhhhtttttttt (that was the air leaving my balloon – total deflation).

I shelved the book before it was even printed.

The book sat in a folder in my email box titled, "Book." For years. Fast forward to Spring, 2024. During a staff retreat, the entire staff as one felt compelled under the Lord to say, "It's time to release the book." It's hard to explain that night. At first, I thought they were being silly, kind, encouraging, only to find the warm weight of the Lord sitting in their words and on their faces. As one they were prophetically showing me an open door that I had closed years prior.

The result of that night is in your hands.

I want to be clear about a few things. Every proceed from this book being sold at illuminate church will go back to the church. I'm not in this for personal gain. The point of the book is to help you learn and then practice what I had to learn, and our family began practicing many moons ago now. Anxiety had put a grip on me. What God taught me and what is shared in this book set me free. Thanks be to God. I hope it helps you or someone you love, too.

Thanks also to my dear and incredibly gifted wife, Christine. (I guess my introduction is now turning into acknowledgements – I told you I don't know what I'm doing!). And to my kids, Owen, Audrey, and Eli. You walked closely with me in the highs and lows of this journey. You were so supportive and leaned into learning how to rest. I know that you know I am not perfect, but when our family is together practicing what we learned, it sure feels perfect. I love you. To my parents, CC and Wallypop. I am what I am because you led me to Jesus. Is there any greater gift a child can receive from his or her parents? You also let me finish this book in the quilt suite. Epic. To the elders and staff of illuminate throughout the years, these pages reflect God's grace to the Ingram family as displayed in your kindness and prayers through our journey. We felt your presence as His presence. I'm so grateful for your faith and lived-out love for Jesus.

To David Stokes who helped transform a message series into a book. You, sir, are a genius (and best-selling author). Please, if you love to read, check out David's books. Google it.

And finally, to the people of illuminate church. When we began illuminate back in 2012, we had no idea what was in store. No idea I would go through this crisis nor the great outcome that has benefitted not just our family, but so many in the church (read on!). It is such a blessing to be the shepherd of a flock of people who are serious about Jesus but have such great joy along the way. Let's keep helping people find abundant life in Jesus. For this reason alone, I have written this book. For Your glory, my King. I love you.

ONE

THE VORTEX OF FEAR

MY WIFE AND I had just experienced one of the greatest "highs" lovers of golf can experience. We'd been in Monterey, California, playing at legendary *Pebble Beach.* It had been as spectacular as you might imagine. If you've never golfed, Pebble Beach is to golfers what Magnolia in Waco, TX is to those with a proclivity for décor and southern charm. Pebble is so very wonderful. That's what makes this next part so strange. I was leaving VACATION! I should have been stress-free and light as a feather off a duckling. Instead, as we were flying back east on the red-eye, I began looking out the window. No big deal. Done it hundreds and hundreds of times. This time? All I could think about was how high I was—how very, terribly, horrifyingly *high* I was.

It was a routine flight like hundreds of others, but as I looked out the window, my mind was increasingly overwhelmed by the empty space between my seat and the good earth. My hands were sweaty, slipping on the armrests as I pushed back in my seat.

My heart was pounding.

Then I felt a sharp pain in my arm, and my panic spiked like it was on steroids. I'd fallen on some stairs while on a visit at my older brother's house. That would have been no big deal except that I'd been carrying my small son, Eli, so I couldn't brace myself and fell hard on one arm. My mind leapt to what someone told me after the injury—I may get *Compartment Syndrome.* If you don't know what that is, neither did I, but it sounded scary, was scary. FYI – I later learned compartment syndrome is a kind of pain that occurs when pressure inside our muscles builds to a dangerous level. It's a very serious condition and just thinking about possibly having an issue I was ignorant of further fueled my sense of dread.

In reality, there was nothing to fear. I was on an ordinary flight with a plane full of calm (i.e., normal) people, but my brain was gyrating between 35,000 feet of emptiness and losing an arm to *Compartment Syndrome*, screaming at me, "You're going to die."

Caught in the vortex of panic, the world shrank around me until I woke up with my head on my wife's lap. I'd sweated through my clothes, and she was stroking my hair saying, roughly interpreted, "Now, now," or possibly, "There, there."

She's nice.

I had a panic attack at 35,000 feet. Passed-out-on-my-wife's-lap type of panic attack. How could this happen to me? I'm a pastor, I follow the PRINCE OF PEACE, and I was returning from vacation. Turns out something was wrong with me that had—to that point—been undetected. I actually had a disease, one that I did not know I had, which *you* might have without knowing. It could be lurking just under the surface of your psyche like a ravenous wolf ready to pounce. My disease had just pounced upon me.

It's called *Accumulated Stress*.

Sometimes something cataclysmic happens that is obviously stressful, and we recognize it and deal with it. But other times, stress comes in a slow creep. We're sinking, almost imperceptibly, the water rising, until it's suddenly lapping at our noses, or right over our heads.

That was what happened to me that day at 35,000 feet.

A routine flight that had never caused me worry before was abruptly, and irrationally, terrifying. And it wasn't the end of the trip. Our plane had to land in Atlanta whereby we had to make a connecting flight to Orlando. I spent the entire time between flights pacing, asking myself, *"How am I ever going to get on this plane? I just can't. Maybe I can rent a car. Or I could walk. Yes, I could just walk home. Anything but this plane."*

My memory is fuzzy about getting on that flight—not to mention cheating death. What a hero am I. When I got home, I almost immediately went to our church Elders. They love their pastor. With them I am free to be my most vulnerable. So, I shared with them what happened. I said, "Guys, listen. I went down hard. I was out hard." Some people talk about peaceful pass-outs. This was not one of those. My brain hurt, my soul hurt—everything hurt.

A door to fear had opened in my life. I could barely preach—not good for a pastor. I even had trouble just standing at the pulpit. I could hardly sleep because I wasn't sure if I was falling asleep or passing out again. You may know exactly what I'm talking about.

I was a mess.

The Elders had advice—a prescription of sorts—for me. They said, "Hey, Tim. The prescription for you is rest, so we're going to put you on sabbatical."

If you're unfamiliar with the term, in the context of a church, a sabbatical is a *rest from ministry*. It's a spiritual discipline, one that is practiced by healthy churches all over the world to refresh and recharge men and women who serve in pastoral roles. We actually have a process of sabbaticals for our pastoral staff at *illuminate church*.

Sabbaticals work.

And the one my elders prescribed worked for me. Kind of. Here's the problem: the sabbatical itself was *reactive* medicine. I was at minus 100 and the sabbatical got me back to zero—just barely living. It didn't handle the basic root issue, which meant without proper soul care, I was going to be right back to that place of unhealth almost as quickly as I had gotten out of it.

Now pay attention here, for the beast lurking in my life was about to be revealed. Four and a half decades, and I'd never known this about myself. Here was the root issue—the thing that had not been dealt with in my life—the reason that I was perpetually stressed, the reason I had a 35,000-foot panic attack: I was in sin. I was living in sin. A pastor, living in sin. WHAT??? What was my sin? I wasn't practicing the *Sabbath.*

You may be thinking, "*Wait. That's it?*"

My kid comes to me crying like the sky has fallen.

"Did you kill the dog?"

"No."

"Did you run over your brother with your bike?"

"No."

"Well, what's wrong?"

"I spilled my water."

"Ummm, ok, no big deal."

That's pretty much how we generally think about breaking the Sabbath. No big deal. But what if I had told you I was committing adultery for years? How would you think about that? To the Lord's heart, committing adultery, murdering, stealing, and lying are all equal to not following the Sabbath. They matter so much to the heart of God because God knows that if we do not follow what He has given us as good life instruction, we will self-destruct.

I did self-destruct. This was my doing. I did not rest, and I paid the price. I did not honor the Sabbath and I reaped the consequences. Here's what's interesting. It was not that I didn't want to rest. On the contrary, I, like most adults, *love* down time. Kids, however, are another story. They resist rest like the plague. Have you ever seen a baby fighting sleep? It's quite remarkable how much they resist dozing off.

But I love *rest* time.

So why didn't I make rest a priority as God commanded? If you had asked me at the time, I might have said I did not have time to rest. But that wasn't actually true. I did not rest because I did not know *how* to rest. Perhaps I'm not the only one who struggles with this. I am pretty sure that the majority of people are a lot like me. The simple fact is, even when we have time to rest, just *how* to make it happen escapes us.

Think about it—when we have a chance for some free time, how many times do we say, "I'm going to do nothing. It's time to take a break!" So we sit on the couch. Then, when we are done "resting," we feel more tired than before, because we've been sitting there as a mere gelatinous blob of flesh. Maybe I reveal too much of myself by saying that. When we get back up, we usually feel worse after "resting."

Or when we are resting, we're thinking of all the things we should be doing or what didn't get done. We actually feel *guilty* for resting because we equate resting to being lazy, instead of getting relaxed and refreshed. As a result, we stop resting and push through whatever task is pressing on our mind. That's the American dream, right? If we work hard enough, we can achieve what we want.

Wrong.

We need to unlearn what we think about rest. And we need to draw close to the Designer's heart to learn what real rest is. Imagine what we could do if we learned to rest the way God designed us to rest. Fully rested, we could charge into our communities with the Good News of Jesus. We could enter our homes and workplaces, being and bringing light and hope to every interaction.

But honestly, this is not how I usually live my life. I'm a pastor, and there are many times I walk into my office and want to say: "Nobody talk to me. I'm beat. Don't bother me. Do *not* disturb. I'm closing the door. I'm gonna sit on my couch—and pray, yeah, that's what I'll be doing!"

I'm pretty sure I'm not alone in this.

Americans are tired all day long and then restless at night. We have no peace during the day, and this turns into poor sleep at night. Our thoughts, stresses, troubles, and fears overtake our hearts and minds.

However, with God's *perfectly-designed* rest, we can know what it means to actually sleep all night. And we can have peace throughout the day, no matter what the circumstances. All we must do is simply follow His design of rest—the way He established it.

You choose. No peace all day and no sleep all night OR know peace all day and know sleep all night.

TWO

THE HINGE-POINT

THE BOOK OF EXODUS in the Bible is the story of how God's people were delivered from 400 years of slavery in Egypt. God led them to the Promised Land so He could make His name famous throughout the Earth. In Exodus chapter 20, God gave the people some guidelines for living. We know them as the Ten Commandments. He basically said, "Live like this and you will have life," because God's vision, will, and plans for life do not hamper life.

They *ensure* it.

God raised up a man named Moses and gave him these directives for His people. Moses brought them to the people so that they could understand how God intended them to live—and how He intends *us* to live, as well. The guidelines are not antiquated. Far from it. They are not old-fashioned.

They are gifts from God.

God said: *"You shall have no other Gods before me."* This is the first commandment. The second one says, *"You shall not make for yourself an idol of any kind or an image of anything in the heavens above or the earth beneath, or in the waters below. You shall not bow down to them or worship them for I, the Lord, your God, am a jealous God, visiting the iniquity of the fathers on their children to the third and fourth generations of those who hate me. But showing loving devotion to 1,000 generations of those who love me and keep my commandments."*

By the way, this means when we bow down to money, to social media, to the mirror, to our wallets, or anything other than God, He regards it as hate speech.

The third commandment says, *"You shall not take the name of the Lord, your God, in vain, for the Lord will not leave anyone unpunished who takes His name in vain."*

Then we come to the fourth one: *"Remember the Sabbath day by keeping it holy. Six days you shall labor and do all your work, but the seventh day is a Sabbath to the Lord your*

God. On it you shall not do any work, neither you, nor your son or daughter, nor your male or female servant, nor you're animals...."

It's the reason cows don't work on Sunday—just ask *Chik-Fil-A.*

"...nor any foreigner residing in your towns. For in six days the Lord God made the heavens and the Earth, the sea, and all that is in them, but He rested on the seventh day. Therefore, the Lord blessed the Sabbath day and made it holy."

The next six commandments round out the celestial list. *"Honor your father and mother so that your days may be long in the land that the Lord, your God, is giving you." "You shall not murder." "You shall not commit adultery." "You shall not steal." "You shall not bear false witness against your neighbor." "You shall not covet your neighbor's house. You shall not covet your neighbor's wife or his male or female servant, his ox or donkey, or anything that belongs to your neighbor."*

Did you notice the emphasis on the fourth commandment? It was, by far, the longest one. One third of all the words in the Ten Commandments have to do with the Sabbath. It's a very revealing fact. You see, for many of us today, that pesky fourth directive is relatively unimportant compared to the other nine. But God put His emphasis right there. If we are to live by "every word" that proceeds from the mouth of God, then when He uses more words, it means more. Sabbath matters to God.

And it should matter to us.

The Sabbath is the *hinge-point* right in the middle of the Ten Commandments. The first commandments tell us that there are no other Gods, we should have no idols, and we should not take the Lord's name in vain. When we honor the Sabbath, we prove that we are honoring and obeying the first three commands. Conversely, if we do not honor the Sabbath, we're really telling God that we are the "lords" of our lives and our time, and that we are going to do what is best according to our thinking, emotion, and will, instead of what God says. When we violate the Sabbath, the first three commandments go out the window. Think about that!

However, when we honor the principle of Sabbath, we not only show that we're following the first three commandments, but we are better able to follow the next six—to honor mother and father, to not murder, to not commit adultery, to not steal, to not lie, to not bear false witness, and to not covet.

If we are honest, many of us struggle with some of these. And it may just be because we are not honoring the Sabbath. You see, in not honoring the Sabbath, we're not allowing God to be the Lord of our lives. We have no strength to obey the Lord because we are not resting in Him and gathering up our strength from Him. Therefore, whatever it is that we are wrestling with is a result of not honoring the Sabbath and not putting God first in our lives.

Do the math.

If life has been hard, we do not need to beat ourselves up. God can replenish, refresh, and restore. This should resonate with us. When we start honoring the Sabbath and actually walking in God's design, aligning with God's heart, imagine how much better all of life can be!

Let's unpack the mystery of this concept we have heard of but perhaps have never really understood. There are four things about the Sabbath that I hope will encourage us to walk with God and consider honoring the Sabbath during our week—every week.

First, the Sabbath was the last thing that God created and the first thing that God made holy.

I love pancakes. I love to make them. I love to eat them. In the Ingram household we have a secret ingredient in our pancakes, one that makes them amazing. Since it is a secret, I cannot reveal what it is. But trust me.

They're great!

When I make pancakes, I always leave enough batter in the bottom of the mixing bowl to make one final enormous monstrosity of a pancake. Does anyone else do this? I like to save the best for last. My kids do not fight over this pancake. This is not because they are kind and generous, although I'm sure they would share that wonderful, big pancake with one another. But the real reason they do not fight over it is because I always eat that pancake before they know it exists. Yep. I save the best for last, and the Lord said, "Let the last be first."

It is my godly duty to eat that pancake *first*.

Maybe this is not the best illustration, but I want us to know that God is a "save the best for last" kind of God. At the beginning of His ministry on earth, Jesus was at a wedding where they ran out of wine. Jesus knew He could help, but when He was first asked, He replied that it was not yet His time. But His mother Mary asked Him to make the wine. So, Jesus made the wine. Note that Jesus was still under the authority of His mother. He obeyed His mom and made the wine. It was the best wine of the night…at the end of the night.

He saved the best for last.

From there Jesus went on to miraculously heal, restore sight, and feed multitudes. He raised the dead. And in the end, He took His own body and went through a gruesome assassination. He went into the tomb and wrestled with the sin of all humanity. He wrestled with the gates of hell, and then a miracle happened. He came back to life. The resurrection of Jesus is the only self-resurrection ever recorded in human history. Everything else was a resuscitation. But Jesus returning to life was a resurrection by His own power.

He saved the best miracle for last.

This is often what we think about creation. God created all of creation in six days, and we often call humanity, what God created on that sixth and final day, the crowning achievement of God's creation. This really is a self-serving narrative, if we think about it. It is so self-centered that even a teenager could figure it out. Here is the truth. We were not the last creation. We were also not the best creation. The Scripture tells us so. In Genesis chapter two, verses one through three, we get the end of the creation story. "*The heavens and the Earth were completed in all their vast array. By the seventh day, God had finished the work He had been doing, so on the seventh day He rested from all His work. Then, God blessed the seventh day and made it holy, because He rested from all the work of creating that He had done.*" God created something on that seventh day. God gave to humanity the Sabbath. In so doing, God created *rest* for all of us.

It was His perfect finishing touch.

When God created the world, He repeatedly pronounced it as *good.* He created the very beginning of the earth, light, sky, land, sea, sun, moon, and stars. He created the sea life, air life, and all of the birds that fly. He declared all of this to be good. On the sixth day, He created everything that walked on the earth. He created animals and then, later in the day, He created *humanity.*

When He created humans, He did not just call that part of creation "good", but He called it *very* good. This is where we get the idea that we are the best part of God's creation. But God was not finished! He had one more thing to create, not because we were not good enough, but because He loved us. What He did next was elevated even above the creation of humanity.

He created rest and He called it *holy.*

Day one: Good. Day two: Good. Day three: Good. Day four: Good. Day five: Good. Day six: Very good. Day seven: Holy. The first thing that God called holy was not a thing. It was not a human. It was a period of time set apart as special to Him.

Sabbath.

This should make us pause and think about what God has intended for the Sabbath. We need to revere it the way that God set it apart to be. Sabbath was the last thing that He created, but the first thing to be called holy.

THREE

JESUS TOOK A NAP

DON'T KNOW HOW to rest? You are in the right place!

The second truth about Sabbath reveals that Sabbath is more about appreciation than recuperation.

This is how God's rest starts to differentiate from ours and where we can begin to learn to rest properly. In order for us to rest, we have to understand how God rests.

I'm sure all of us have had the experience of an extremely tiring day. Probably countless times. Not necessarily a day where we slept poorly, or simply a very busy and stressful day. I'm talking about one of those days when we exerted ourselves to the limit and just collapsed at the end. Like a long day of strenuous yard work, when the yard needed trimming, flowers needed planting, hedges needed work, and lawn needed mowing. When we were finally finished, we looked like we went swimming because our clothes were soaked with sweat.

Or what about the time that we helped a friend move. Why does furniture owned by our friends tend to seem heavier than our own? And why do they always have to live on the sixth floor? It's so hard. Exhausting. Or that time when we waited for what seemed like eternity in a long line for Flight of Passage at *Disney World.* (Note: our faith community is right outside Disney in Kissimmee, Florida. People do voluntarily wait an inordinate amount of time for this ride depicting the world from the movie *Avatar.* Dangerous of me to say here, but it's not worth the wait!) Yard work, moving, long lines...they all end in our need to rest. But how?

Isaiah 40:28 says, "*He neither faints, nor is weary,*" yet He rested. Wait, if God rests though He never tires, even while creating all of creation, His rest must be different than ours. There must be a different purpose or method. There must be something that He is doing that we have not yet understood.

One of the Hebrew words for rest is "menuchah." It's pronounced "ma-new-ah." Not manure. It means restfulness that is also a celebration. Resting by celebrating. What? We so often think that resting takes place on the couch with bonbons and football (don't judge) or binging something on Netflix.

In Exodus chapter 13, before the Ten Commandments were given, the Lord said to Moses, "Consecrate to me every firstborn male. The first offspring of every womb among the Israelites belongs to me whether human or animal." Then Moses told the people to commemorate that day. To mark that day aside as special.

That day was the day they came out of Egypt.

They had been in Egypt for 430 years, the latter part as slaves building things for the Egyptians under horrific conditions. They were to commemorate the day they came out of Egypt, out of the land of slavery, because the Lord brought them out with a mighty hand. *"When the Lord brings you into the land of the Canaanites, Hittites, Amorites, Hivites, and Jebusites—the land He swore to your ancestors to give you, a land flowing with milk and honey—You are to observe this ceremony in this month. For seven days, eat bread made without yeast and on the seventh day hold a festival to the Lord."* On the seventh day, celebrate. On the seventh day, celebrate because you are appreciating what He has redeemed you from: the hand of slavery.

Rest means we appreciate. Rest means we celebrate. God was not refreshed in His rest because He sat down and drank some Gatorade and took a hot shower. God was refreshed by taking joy from the very work that He accomplished.

Rest is finishing the yard work and looking over the yard and appreciating the finished product. It's idyllic. "Look what we did!" It's the moment when we finish helping our friends move, and we take a step back to say, "Whew, I'm so glad that is done." It's the sense of achievement we have knowing that our friends are settling into their new home. Rest is getting through the line of Flight of Passage and finally enjoying the ride! Actually, when I finally rode Flight of Passage, I immediately felt like hurling into a trash can. It was intense!

The point is that God's rest is a celebration. When God created us, He did not say, "Wow, that was a lot of work! I'm exhausted." God made us, took a step back to look at us and said, "It is very good." Read that again.

Then, He rested.

God's pleasure at His work recharged Him. God Sabbathed. He rested. He appreciated His work. He was pleased with His work. God created our co-workers, in-laws, people of all skin colors, people of all faiths, and people who are different than we are. His creation does not always live in the way He intended them to live, but He is still pleased with His work.

Are we?

If we Sabbath, we might be. Maybe racial reconciliation happens in a church where people are Sabbathing. Maybe marriages come together at a high rate in homes where the people are Sabbathing. Appreciating and celebrating what God has created (even appreciating "different" people, maybe especially "different" people) is a great part of the Sabbath.

When we Sabbath, we are thanking God for our spouses, co-workers, and the Muslim man who keeps trying to convert us to his faith. We appreciate. We celebrate. Our thinking and our desires start to line up with God's intention in us.

So firstly, God saved the best for last in the Sabbath, and secondly, the Sabbath is not a celebration of rest as much as it is rest via celebration.

Third, the Sabbath makes us *still*. For most of us it is hard to sit still for five minutes. Psalm 23 is probably the most famous passage of scripture. Or possibly a close second to John 3:16. In that popular Psalm, David wrote about the Great Shepherd. Verse two says, *"He makes me to lie down in green pastures. He leads me beside still waters."*

Here is that Hebrew word for still again, "*menuchah*." Also again, not manure. God leads us to *restful* waters. He leads us to a place where we can drink in appreciation. Where we can drink in celebration. Through drinking the water, we are recharged and reenergized, simply thanking God for who He is and what He has done for us.

It's the feeling we have after a time of worship. Imagine if that feeling, that appreciation of who God is, was extended through a whole day? We simply say, "Lord, I am in your presence. I am walking with You, and I am so overjoyed because of who You are and what You have done in my life." This is a correct understanding of Sabbath. So, what does stillness look like? The Shepherd wants to lead us by the still waters. Who remembers the old saying, "You can lead a horse to water, but you can't make it DRINK?" The Lord wants to lead us to the still waters, but it is up to us to drink.

The book of Mark is an account of what Jesus did while He was on the Earth. And in chapter four of that Gospel, we find an incredible story. In verse 35 we read that when evening came Jesus said to His disciples, *"Let's go to the other side."* Jesus had a vision. He said, "This is the plan. We are moving from here to there."

Verse 36 says that they left the crowd behind and took Jesus along in the boat. There were also other boats with them. A furious squall came up. Imagine the *Deadliest Catch*. The waves broke over the boat so that it was nearly swamped.

Jesus was in the stern of the boat, sleeping on a cushion. The disciples woke Him and said, *"Teacher, don't you care if we drown?"* So, Jesus got up and rebuked the wind. He said to the waves, *"Quiet! Be still."* The wind immediately died down, and it was completely calm. Remember, Jesus had already told them where they were going. They were going to the other side. If Jesus said they were going to the other side, then you better believe, they were going to the other side! But something came up along the way to their destination.

Between them and their goal was a potential disaster.

How many of us have experienced this in our own lives? God gives us a plan, a path, a destination. We start out in the direction that He lays out for us. Suddenly a storm comes up. Life happens. We start to doubt God. We start to doubt His plan, His direction for our lives. This is what the disciples experienced.

And right in the middle of their freak-out session, Jesus took a nap.

Here is the promise of the Sabbath: If Jesus can lay down in the middle of the storm and rest, so can we. In fact, so should we. He has already told us where we are going. He has given us direction through His Word and through the guidance of Holy Spirit. There is nothing that can stop what is going to happen because the Lord has spoken.

As a result, I choose to lay down and rest with my Savior. I'm going to ride to the other side and have faith. I'm going to skip the freak-out session. I'm going to skip the panic attack at 35,000 feet because I choose to rest with my Savior. Wouldn't it be great if we could get to this point? Where we can take a nap with Jesus, even in the middle of the storm because we KNOW that He is in control? We can be still. We can Sabbath.

FOUR

PUT A RING ON IT

THE FOURTH ENCOURAGING *thing about Sabbath is that it cures aloneness.*

All of us need to get married today. Every single one of us, no matter our age. If you are young. If you are old. If you are already married. If you are single. If you are divorced. If you are remarried for the fourth time. All of us reading this book need to be married today. No, I don't mean literally as husband and wife.

Well then, what do I mean?

In the creation account in Scripture, we read that on the sixth day, man was lacking, so God created woman. He said it is not suitable for man to be alone, nor for a woman to be alone, if the order had been reversed. It is not good for a person to be alone. God created the perfect alternative. One to the other, man and woman. But guess what?

They still lacked.

If they had everything they needed, God would have been finished. The story would have ended after six days. But humanity still lacked, so there was a seventh day. God gave man something else. He gave the Sabbath. He gave rest. And in so doing, He gave us communion with Him. He gave oneness with Him by spending a day of our week with Him. Remember, God said in Genesis 3:3, *"God made this Sabbath time holy."* He declared, *"It is holy."* Then God told man in the Ten Commandments to honor the Sabbath and keep it holy. The way we keep the Sabbath holy is by *marrying* it.

Put a ring on it.

The Bible says in Ephesians chapter five, *"Husbands, love your wives just as Christ loved the church and gave Himself up for her, to make her holy, cleansing her by the washing with water through the Word, and to present her to Himself as a radiant church without stain or wrinkle or any other blemish, but holy and blameless."* God married the church by giving

His life to the church, by literally being sacrificed on the cross and washing us through His blood, through the forgiveness of our sins. Then He told the men, *"Husbands, do the same for your wives."*

Now let's be clear. Jesus was not saying that men make women holy. Jesus alone makes us holy. But He was telling us that man's duty is to not lead their wives into sin. To do this, men must also stay away from sin. If the man is in sin, he will lead his wife into sin. Not only should husbands not lead wives into sin, but they should be leading them TO God. Because God alone sanctifies. God alone makes us holy. Husbands, do not lead your wives towards sin but towards holiness.

When I am asking us to marry the Sabbath, I'm simply asking us to look at one day of our week and say, "God, I'm not going to lead this day into sin. I'm not going to do what I have done every other day." This will look different to different people. It may mean we literally and physically do things differently. We will watch our mouths. We will keep our thoughts pure. We are going to keep ourselves holy, devoted to God, on this day.

On this Sabbath day we are going to give ourselves and the entire day to the Lord. This is what it means to "marry the Sabbath." We make it a day set apart. We make it a day we are uniquely, wonderfully tied together with Jesus.

When we marry the Sabbath, and we honor and practice it, God will purify us. He will break off chains that bind us, allowing us to have intimacy with God. Oneness. A constant abiding with the Lord, our God. A tangible presence of God.

In other words, every week we get to have a perfect day with God.

Take a moment to remember a perfect day in your life. Maybe it was with your spouse and kids. Maybe it was with a friend. Maybe it was an amazing day of time spent alone.

My wife and I recently had a perfect day. We were on a ministry trip in Scottsdale, Arizona. We were meeting with pastors from all over the country, relating with them, learning from them, and praying with them. It was an incredible trip, with opportunities to share and to grow.

Before the scheduled conference events started, the ministry network we were a part of gifted us with an extra night, which means we got there a day early. That first morning we woke up and ordered room service, which was a real treat for us. The people from the resort came and set the breakfast out on the balcony. It overlooked a golf course, mountains, and cacti. The temperature was perfect (about 70 degrees). The sun was shining in a clear, blue sky.

Perfection.

After our perfect breakfast, we went hiking. Now that may not be everyone's idea of perfection, but it is for us. It was a hard, arduous climb. It seemed like it was straight up. We were breathing heavily. We had to stop frequently to drink water. We took our time and made our way up the mountain. It took a long time. But there was this moment when we reached the top where it seemed like we could see forever. We saw mountain ranges that went on and on, and the glory of God was right there in front of us.

It was amazing. Perfect.

Later that night, we went to dinner at a place that the hotel suggested. It was called Tonto Bar and Grill. When we got there, we found a tiny restaurant that was not very impressive. There was very little seating. It was cramped. The ceilings were low. But it had great reviews, so we told the host that we would like a table for two. To our surprise, the host led us through the dining room and out to a back patio that we did not previously see. It was on a golf course overlooking the 18th green.

Have I told you that golf is my love language?

There were cacti everywhere. I looked at my wife, who is one of the most beautiful women in the world. And that night, sitting under the stars, she looked like an angel.

We had an amazing night. We had a great conversation. We laughed. The food was exquisite. It was just, well, perfect. It was a perfect day. We had spent the entire day communing with each other, from start to finish. Enjoying each other. Celebrating each other.

Our perfect day is a picture of what happens when we marry the Sabbath. When we spend the perfect day with the Lord, our God, I promise that we will find intimacy with Him that we thought was reserved for Mother Theresa and Billy Graham. It is for us. We will walk with Him. We will talk with Him and hear from Him.

As it was always intended.

Imagine, in the cool of the evening, in the garden with the Lord, our God, our Creator, we can rest with Him, celebrate with Him. We can tell Him how much we appreciate the things, big and small, that He has taken care of in our lives. When we have communion with Him one day a week, our lives are changed in the other six. And then God gives us another chance on the seventh day to do it all over again. He wants to give us a perfect day with Him. He wants to kill aloneness in our lives by becoming our best friend and the love of our lives. We can walk with Him, talk with Him, sing with Him, and rejoice with Him.

We can have true fellowship with Him.

FIVE

FOR GOODNESS' SAKE

MANY OF US have grown up in the faith. We were raised in church. We've been around long enough to know the lingo, the "*Christianese*." We throw around secretly sanctified words and phrases and expect everyone to know what we're talking about. We talk "traveling mercies" or "tithing" or "a hedge of protection"—stuff like that. They roll off our tongues with ease and fall flat in front of people trying to discover Jesus, or even church *newbies*.

The word "Sabbath" could fall into this category. If I were not a Christian, I would have no idea what Sabbath means. Is it like a warm bath? A hot bath? A sab bath? As you read, I do not want to assume that everyone understands what I'm talking about. In fact, I would dare say that even those of us who have been exposed to things of the Lord for a long time could use a periodic refresher course on what Sabbath really means to us and for us.

As I do my best to unpack the meaning and implication of Sabbath, it is easier said than done. There is so much to it. It cannot be explained in one quick, crisp, cute definition. That would be like trying to explain Jesus in one sentence. Impossible. In Sabbath there is texture. There is life. There is depth. But in its plainest and most general sense, *Sabbath is one twenty-four-hour period that is set aside each week to commune with God. A day to rest from our normal work and focus on the goodness of God.*

Goodness.

What is the goodness of God? What does it mean to focus on the goodness of God? Does it mean meditation? Does it mean that in order to practice the Sabbath I must live like a monk once a week? No. Now, certainly God can call us to incorporate meditation and elements of a monastic lifestyle during Sabbath, but these are not requirements.

Relieved?

Because if we are honest, those things aren't toe-tappers to most of us.

The Sabbath is simply focusing on the goodness of God for 24 hours. Celebrating the goodness of God. We focus on the things that God has given us that bring us joy in life. For many of us it is family. We can do that on our Sabbath. For many of us it is friends. We can focus on our friends during the Sabbath. God gave us our family and friends. He is pleased when we "enjoy" what He has given us. So, we honor the things that He has given us.

We can also focus on the goodness of God by focusing on *ourselves*. It's not self-centered for us to do some self-care on the Sabbath, as long as that self-care is directed toward the Lord. If we enjoy gardening, we can work in the garden. On the Sabbath we are told to rest from our *normal* work. If working in the garden, surrounded by God's glorious nature gives us life, then we absolutely should enjoy it! Conversely, if working in the garden is a chore that we detest, we should definitely not do it on the Sabbath. NO CHORES!

Take a nap.

Go to the beach.

Read a good book.

Talk to a child.

Take a drive.

Crank up the worship music and run around the house in your underwear like King David did.

But only if you are home alone.

Enjoying the goodness of God, whatever brings you life, is the purpose of Sabbath. Twenty-four hours dedicated to God. It's a gift from God, born out of His love for us. We return that love to Him by enjoying the gifts that He, the greatest gift, has given us.

We enjoy Him most of all.

In Exodus 20:8, God commands us to *"Remember the Sabbath Day by keeping it Holy. Six days you shall labor and do all your work, but the seventh day is a Sabbath to the Lord your God, in which you must not do any work. Neither you nor your son or daughter, nor your manservant, your maidservant, your livestock, nor the foreigner within your gates. For in six days the Lord made the heavens and the earth and the sea and all that is in them. But on the seventh day, God rested. Therefore, the Lord blessed the Sabbath day and set it apart as holy."*

Remember, God commands us to rest. It is not just a suggestion. God's rest is different than our rest. We need to learn to rest the way God rested. God commands us to rest as He rested for our benefit.

I went to the University of Florida. Steve Spurrier Field in Gainesville, Florida, otherwise known as "The Swamp," is the home of the *Gators*. The stadium is very tall. When I attended the university, I was part of the university's Army ROTC program. One day, as part of our training, we rappelled down the side of the stadium. That's basically going over the edge and scaling down the outside wall connected only to a rope and a harness. Fun.

We walked up to the top of the stadium. Our commanding sergeants had everything set up. They had the whole area belayed off, which is a fancy way of saying all the ropes were safely tied off. We had to go over the edge. GULP. The entire morning, as one by one we rappelled over and down the side of the stadium, those army sergeants gave us orders. They told us how and when to lean, how quickly to go, etc. If we chose not to follow their careful and wise instructions, we could have conceivably faced death. It was that simple.

Obey or die.

Obedience is not only good—it's *smart*.

Several years ago, I attended a pastor's conference, in Dallas, Texas. I met and learned from many incredible pastors who have done awesome things for the Lord. During the conference, three of these pastors were on a panel, teaching us how to be better leaders in ministry. Three heavy-weights in the ministry world sat facing us ready to dispense their wisdom. I had pen in hand ready to gather as much wisdom as God was about to share through these leaders.

The moderator asked this question: "What do you remember about the early years of the church? Not like the book of Acts, but when you first started *your* church. What do you remember about the first couple of years?"

The first pastor, a very astute man with a great sense of humor, answered, "I remember the meetings. Meetings with people. Investing vision. Injecting people with life. Encouraging and inviting people to come on the journey with me."

The next pastor answered, "I remember creating DNA and culture."

Both men answered with memories of the organizational and visionary work.

I was eating it up. I must do meetings! I must cast vision and hold fast to a healthy culture to ensure LIFE in every area of illuminate church. Ok! I'm getting it.

But then the last pastor answered. His answer was very different. "I remember the warfare," he said. I could feel the atmosphere change from light to heavy, because we all knew that he nailed it. I got goosebumps feeling the reality of this great truth.

Spiritual warfare is real.

Not long after that conference, my family and I went through the greatest season of spiritual warfare we have ever experienced. There were health issues in our family, a very difficult staff transition that I had to lead through, and then of course, my own bout of anxiety that began at 35,000 feet. This season was caused by the devil who hates us and wants to destroy the church. The spiritual warfare mounted against us attempted to prevent our family and the church from going forward. But praise be to God, the gates of hell will not prevail against the church—in Jesus' name! That deserves a hallelujah.

The Lord commands us in His word to be alert and sober-minded, for our enemy, the devil, prowls around like a roaring lion, seeking whom he may devour. The Lord gives us a command. He says, "Be alert." It's a command, not a suggestion. If we do not want to fall prey to the devil's schemes, we must be sober-minded. God's commands give us life. They protect our lives. They preserve our lives. And God commanded us to rest. He commanded us to remember the Sabbath, and to keep it holy, set apart for Him. Obey or die. I found out the hard way. What about you?

SIX

A TALE OF TWO WATCHES

IN THE BOOK of Deuteronomy, we read about God's law. In fact, the name, Deuteronomy, basically means, second law or "law again." This is because it is actually the second book of the Bible that details God's law. The first was the book of Leviticus.

In the book of Deuteronomy, Moses presented the law to the people right before they were going to enter the promised land. The people had been enslaved in Egypt before God delivered them from the cruel hands of

Pharaoh. This deliverance of the people was followed by forty years of wandering in the wilderness, because of their sin. Now, they were finally preparing to cross the Jordan River and enter the Holy Land.

It is for this reason in Deuteronomy Moses recounted to the people the Law of God before they entered the Promised Land. In Deuteronomy 30:11, God said to them, *"Now what I am commanding you today is not too difficult for you or beyond your reach."* This is very interesting. He said it to the people of Israel, and I believe that He is saying it to us today.

In other words, we do not have to have a seminary degree or a Ph.D. to understand and follow God's commands. There is not a level of growth in the church that we have to achieve before we can follow God's ways. Note, these easy-to-follow commands included the one about rest. The passage goes on to say, *"It is not up in heaven so that you have to ask who will ascend into heaven to get it and proclaim it to us so we may obey it. Nor is it beyond the sea that you have to ask who will cross the sea to get it and proclaim it to us so that we may obey it. No, the Word is very near you. It is in your mouth and in your heart so you may obey it."*

He is talking to me. He is talking to us. *"See I set before you today, life and prosperity or death and destruction, for I command you today to love the Lord your God, to walk in obedience to Him, and to keep His commands, His decrees, and His laws. Then you will live and increase, and the Lord your God will bless you in the land you are entering to possess. But if your heart turns away and you are not obedient, and if you are drawn away to bow down to other gods and worship them, (i.e. yourself) I declare to you this day that you will certainly be destroyed. You will not live long in the land you are crossing the Jordan to enter and possess. This day, I call the heavens and the earth as witnesses against you that I have set before you life and death, blessings and curses. Now choose life so that you and your children may live and that you may love the Lord your God, listen to His voice, and hold fast to Him. For the Lord is your life, and He will give you many years in the land He swore to give your fathers, Abraham, Isaac, and Jacob."*

Now choose life.

When we look at a watch, what do we see? Do we see the beautiful dial, the numbers, the hands that are so faithful and intricate? Does it remind us that "this is the day that the Lord has made. Let us rejoice and be glad in it?" Or does it make us think that time is running short? Does it remind us of all we have to do? Hurry up. Time is ticking away.

Let me introduce two different watches. They represent our perception. Our attitudes. Our point of view. It is up to us which watch we choose to put on each day.

I call the first watch the *death watch*. It's based on a Greek word found in the Bible—*chronos*. It is the root of words like chronology and chronological. It has to do with dates, calendars, and portions of time. We find *chronos* in John 5:5-6. *"One man there had been an invalid for 38 years."* A period of time. *"When Jesus saw him lying there and realized that he had spent a long time (chronos) in this condition, He asked him, 'Do you want to get well?'"*

Thirty-eight years—a period of time that had elapsed. *Chronos* is time marching on. It's time running out. *Chronos* is our kids growing up too fast. *Chronos* is looking in the mirror and seeing wrinkles that weren't previously there. *Chronos* is getting older. Eventually it is chronos that catches up to us. We ponder and dread our future and our physical death. *Chronos* is time coming to get us. I am running out of time!

The second type of watch is the *life watch*. It is based on another Greek word—*kairos*.

Kairos is a moment or a season of moments. The word appears many times in scripture. In Mark 1:15, Jesus says, "'*The time (kairos) has come, The Kingdom of God has come near. Repent and believe the good news.*'" Mark 13:32-33 says, "*but about that day or hour no one knows, not even the angels in heaven nor the Son, but only the Father. Be on guard. Be alert. You do not know when that time (kairos) will come.*"

Literally translated, Kairos means, "time as opportunity." Wow. Let that sink in. Time as opportunity. When we view time in this manner, we value what is happening right here and right now. We focus on what is right in front of us. We stay present in each and every moment. We do not live in fear of the future. We do not live in regret of the past. We appreciate each scene of life and every season of life for what it is. Each moment is a gift from God. Instead of despairingly saying, "I only have 45 years left," the person who is living according to the *life watch* excitedly says, "I still have 45 years of life left! God, what else do you have in store for me?" The person who lives according to kairos sees every moment as a sovereign gift from God, ordained of God.

In the movie The Matrix, the main character, Neo, is offered the opportunity to leave the perception that he believes is real to discover the true reality. According to the movie, the matrix is the reality where crazy things happen behind what can normally be seen to a humanity ignorant of the truth. Neo is offered the real truth. All he has to do to know the truth is to take a little red pill. If he chooses the red pill, he will be catapulted down into the wormhole to discover a reality he could never have imagined. But Neo is also offered a blue pill. If he chooses to take the blue pill he will be returned to normal life, with no memory of the truth of the matrix. He will go back to living in ignorance.

Neo chooses the red pill.

The *death watch* is like taking the blue pill. We just stay in the norm of what we know. We are born. We go to school. We may get married. We may have children. We pay taxes. We grow old. We die. That is chronos. One segment of life after another, we go on punching the card. We live in the routine. One foot in front of the other. All the way to the very end. There is no notice of sovereignty. No recognition of divinity. Simply doing life as it comes.

The *life watch* is like taking the red pill. It is a revelation of an entire new world. It is a world in which time is redeemed. Every moment of our life is redeemed as a life-giving opportunity from God. Every moment, every season is redeemed by God. In his book, *The Rest of God*, Mark Buchanan says, "Kronos is time we waste, and Kairos is time we seize."

My son, Owen, was seventeen years old when I wrote this book. He was a high school senior and would soon be graduating and leaving home. As his parents, my wife and I could have looked at this moment in two ways. If we chose to look at it like the *death watch* we would have said, "Please God, can he live with us forever? We do not want him to leave!" We would focus on the negative, knowing that our time with him is coming to an end, dwelling on how much we are going to miss him, and all that we are going to lose when he goes.

However, if we chose the *life watch*, we would have said, "God, thank You for the precious gift of our son. Every moment that we have had with him has been a blessing." We would choose to see every moment as sovereign from God. We would recognize that there is a moment when God asks us to release him into his own destiny, so that God can do what He is going to do in our son's life. The bird has to leave the nest in order to fly. It is meant to be.

My wife, Christine, and I met our good friend, Dennis Walker, in 2007, when we moved to The Crossing Church in Tampa, Florida. Dennis, or Denny as we call him, was one of the Elders at the church. Denny is an amazing man of God. He and his wife, Beverly, had two daughters, Hannah and Andrea. Hannah used to babysit our kids when they were younger. Andrea, their oldest daughter, was tragically killed in a car accident on February 11, 1999.

When I learned about the tremendous loss that Denny had lived through, I was amazed. I saw a man who served as an Elder in the church. A man who believed God. A man who walked with God. A man who trusted God. I told him he was amazing, that I admired and respected him seeing how he was able to carry on after the tragedy.

Denny then told me that it was not always the case. You see, I met Denny eight years after he lost his daughter. I met him after years of healing. But what Denny shared with me was that when his daughter died he was plunged into a darkness that he could not even explain. For nearly two years, he contemplated taking his own life, almost daily. He admits that he would have, but he did not have the courage to do it. He was so overcome with sorrow and grief.

One day he read a verse that he had read many times before, but that day it spoke to him and got his attention. *"This day, I call the heavens and earth as witnesses against you that I have set before you life and death, blessings and curses."* Sound familiar? Denny said it was as if the voice of Heaven boomed down to him. Denny felt that God was telling him to choose life, to choose to live, to choose to see God's glory. God helped him to choose to have a moment when God redeemed an awful tragedy. Denny made a choice to not live by the chronos watch of death, but the kairos watch of life. He chose to see that both the wonderful things and awful things that happen can be used for the glory of God, if we will see it as such.

Denny said that, for him, life was facing God. Death was turning his back on God. For two years Denny had sat with his back to the Lord. He was angry, broken, bitter, and full of grief. But then God told him to choose life and turn his face toward Him. God walked through it with him. Denny made the switch and came back to abundant life with God.

In the movie *Shawshank Redemption*, Red says, "Get busy living, or get busy dying." God wants us to get busy living.

Some of us, like Denny, have faced great loss in our lives. Grief is a natural process that must be gone through. We do not just "get over it." But in proper perspective, through healing in God's time, we can live again. Life can be restored again. It is possible.

Some of us may be in a season of sitting with our backs toward God. We are opposed to God because of something that has happened to us, or something we have done. We doubt His love for us. We hide from God. But God tells us that there is no need to hide. He has set before us life and death, blessings and curses. We can choose to live. We can choose to live in His rest.

When we practice the Sabbath we are choosing life. We see everything through the perspective of God's heart and God's eyes. It changes the way we think, the way that we live, the way that we care for others and for ourselves. Every moment becomes significant. When we practice the Sabbath, God resets the watch of our lives to His *life watch.*

SEVEN

UNUSED VACATION DAYS

THE FIRST TIME my younger brother broke his arm, we were visiting my grandparents in El Paso, Texas. I have an older brother, Matt, and a younger brother, Fred. Matt was roughhousing with us younger brothers, as older brothers do. We had this game where he would lay on the ground on his back and use his legs to launch us into the air. Sounds safe, right? Over and over we would do this. Launch and land. Launch and land. Then Matt launched Fred extremely high. When he landed, he landed with his body on his arm. I still remember that his arm looked like an S. Barf. When they got to the hospital, the doctor had to re-break his arm to set it so that it could properly heal.

The second time Fred broke his arm, it was my fault. We were living in Germany because my dad was in the military. We were outside playing on the clothesline. Fred was swinging, hanging from the pole that held up the clothesline. He asked me to help him stop swinging and get down. He was about to lose his grip. So, I grabbed his legs and held on. He told me if I didn't let him go, he would fall. So, I let him go. And he fell anyway. Hard. I looked down at him lying on the ground. The S in his arm was back. Barf again.

Later, after Fred had his cast on, we had a rare, nice, brother-to-brother moment. I told him I was sorry for breaking his arm. He told me that the fall itself didn't hurt that much. It was when they once again had to re-set his arm that it hurt so badly. But in the long run, my brother was glad that they had, because it was the re-set that allowed his arm to heal properly.

Just as the doctors were able to re-set my brother's arm, so God designed the Sabbath to reset our souls so they can be healthy and function properly. It's the break that fixes us. Follow me here…

As I was doing research about the Sabbath and rest, I came across a lot of scientific information about rest, and some striking statistics. From 1978 to 2000 our country used to take a great amount of time for vacation, averaging about 20.3 days each year. After 2000 there was a large decrease in used vacation days, only averaging 17.4 in 2018. Americans do not use 29% of their vacation days, which in 2018 equaled 768 million unused vacation days. That's a lot of missed opportunities!

The term workaholic was coined in the early 1900s. Most of us are familiar with the term—people who put too much life into their work at the expense of the rest of life. You may not believe this, but the term was first introduced in an article about ministers!!!! The first time the term workaholism was used was to describe the work habits of people, it was describing people in ministry. The people who are supposed to be most connected to God and resting with God the most were doing it the worst!

Here is what science has told us about the effects of rest. A four-day vacation will refresh us for four weeks. After just four weeks, our bodies will need another rest. Many of us take one big summer vacation each year. Or, if we are lucky, maybe a trip every six months. Yet, according to science, we would need thirteen four-day vacations per year to stay in a great place, mentally, emotionally, and physically. If we do the math, we see that four days of rest thirteen times per year multiplies to fifty-two days of rest needed per year. But we are only using 17.4 days. No wonder we are stressed, burnt out, exhausted, and even dying at alarming rates.

Did you catch that? We are missing the mark of fifty-two days of rest. Science has shown us that fifty-two days of rest per year are needed to keep us in a healthy state. I find it very interesting that there are fifty-two Sabbaths commanded by God per year. One Sabbath per week equals fifty-two days of rest. God already knew what science is only now discovering. We need the rest that God created and designed.

Can we imagine going on a vacation already rested? Imagine starting a vacation from a place of rest, instead of stressed and looking for an escape from life. We would enjoy it more. We are so exhausted on vacation that we cannot enjoy it until it is almost time to go back home. Back to work…and unrest.

God loves us so much that He commands us to rest. Through this command He tells us that every moment is a gift from Himself. He wants us to set aside one day per week to remind us to truly live. If we are willing to see it, we will acknowledge that there are ordained moments in which He has brought about incredible intersections that radically, peaceably, and wonderfully inspire and fulfill us.

How are we responding to God's command to rest? I believe we usually respond in one of three ways. First, we may respond like a toddler. When parents ask a toddler to rest, they fight it. They cry. They resist. They fuss. They may get violent. And then they finally collapse out of sheer exhaustion and frustration.

Second, we may respond like an adult. As adults, many times we want to rest for escape. We wake up in the morning, and immediately wish we could stay in bed all day. We want to fall into sleep so that we do not have to think about the worries and stress of our days and our lives. But God did not give us rest to escape life. On the contrary, He gave us rest so that we can enjoy and experience life.

The third, and possibly the best way we respond to God's command to rest is as a baby. Babies have the ability to take a sweet nap in the arms of a loved one, no matter the commotion around them. They do not fight it. They are not trying to escape and hide. They are able to rest easily in the arms of a loving parent. This is a picture of what God wants from us. He wants us to be able to rest in His loving arms, provision, and protection, no matter the circumstances of life.

EIGHT

FIGHT VS. FLIGHT

I TRULY BELIEVE that if we set aside a 24-hour period for God, each week, He will take the remaining six days and do more with them than we can possibly imagine.

God can *always* do more with less.

As I was learning, studying, and writing about the Sabbath, I would occasionally use the word "Sabbathing." It's not actually a word, but I have made it one, and I use it. It's the verb of doing the Sabbath. Sabbathing. When I write the word, Sabbathing, into my computer, a funny thing happens. It autocorrects the word.

Sunbathing.

At first, I got annoyed every time it happened. But then I thought about it. Sunbathing. Isn't that really what the Sabbath is? God used autocorrect to correct my thinking. Forgive me for a moment of pastoral cheesiness.

Sunbathing = S-O-N bathing.

To bathe in the Son. Glory to God.

Most of us are familiar with the story of *Chicken Little*. This chicken believed the world was going to end. He declared over and over again, "The sky is falling, the sky is falling!" He worried. He stressed. The spirit that he displayed in the story is a spirit that is sadly familiar to many of us.

The spirit of *exasperation*.

It's that moment when we cry over spilt milk. When we have a flat tire. When we're facing another bad diagnosis, another bill, another problem. Every time that something comes, we clench. Sadly, we tend to live our lives like this, tightly wound. Clinched. My prayer is that Sabbath will help us put this spirit of exasperation to death.

We've all heard the term, "flight or fight." Which one do you identify with? Are you a fighter? Or are you a flighter? (Another made up word). If something comes up do you fight? (A fighter). Or is your impulse to run or hide? (A flighter). Growing up, I was a flighter.

I remember a time when I was a child living in Kansas. One day, my family decided to have a yard sale. My father was in the army, so we moved around a lot. There were many yard sales over the years. We used a small cardboard pencil box to hold the money from sales. This particular day we must have been making some great sales because I remember the money box being full of small bills. A gust of wind hit, and suddenly it was raining money. Money everywhere. Now, most people would react by chasing and collecting the money. Me?

I freaked out.

I exasperated.

I ran.

I was *Chicken Little*.

I have another memory from childhood about my brother, Fred. We were roller-skating near my grandparents' pool in El Paso, Texas. You guessed it. He went right in the pool, with the equivalent of lead weights on his feet. I ran. I freaked out.

Don't worry. He was fine.

Then, when I was 16 years old, I had a 1976 *Mazda GLC* hatchback. I called it the rust bucket. Because it was. One day I went into the garage, got into the rust bucket, put it in reverse, and hit the gas until I was stopped by a loud boom. Now, normally, there was no vehicle parked *behind* my car. But on that day my father had borrowed a truck and parked it behind the rust bucket. I hit it hard. What did I do? Did I go inside and confess what had happened? Nope. I got out of the car. I walked to the sidewalk.

And I ran. I was a flighter.

Fight or flight are both responses to fear stimuli. They are gifts from God. He gave us these instincts for a reason. And there are appropriate times to use each of these God-given instincts.

The problem arises when fight or flight becomes an addiction, a lifestyle.

Most Americans live habitually in fight or flight. We live in a constant state of exasperation, like *Chicken Little*. We need to kill that chicken. You see, both reactions—fight and flight—leave us exhausted. The mechanism that is supposed to bring us to safety becomes the very thing that causes us harm. With each battle, our response leaves us more and more worn out, so when another battle emerges, we have nothing left to give. We have no more fight in us. And we have no energy for flight. We just lay down and take it.

We need to rethink fight vs. flight.

Most of us have heard of the Biblical prophet Isaiah. The word prophet means *I hear from God, and I speak the words I hear.* That is what a prophet does. In fact, in Isaiah chapter 30, the very words we read from Isaiah say, *"This is what God says."* He is a prophet.

Telling what God says is his function. So, what does God want us to hear?

Isaiah 30:15-16 says, *"This is what the Sovereign Lord, the Holy One of Israel says, 'In repentance and rest is your salvation.'"* Repentance means to change the way that we think. We have been thinking with a fight or flight mentality, and the Lord is telling us to change the way we think. There is a new way to rest, and this way is our salvation and quietness.

Trust is our strength.

Pay attention to the next seven words in this passage. "But you would have none of it." This passage was written thousands of years ago to the people of Israel, but I believe that it is equally applicable to most Americans today. Indeed all of humanity. God says that He is offering repentance and rest, but we are so busy and so plugged in (hello smartphones) to everything that is going on around us that we refuse His rest. That is what verse 16 says about the Israelites. They said, "No, this is what we are going to do, God. We are going to flee on horses." And God says, "Therefore you will flee. You've made a declaration in your spirit and that is exactly what you are going to do." The Israelites told God that instead of repenting and taking His rest, they would ride off on fast horses. But God tells them that their pursuers will be swift. In other words, they can run all they want, but these problems will catch up with them sooner or later.

Just like the Israelites, we are trying to fight or flee from our problems. But the problems are not going anywhere. They keep coming. They overtake us.

But God offered His people another option to fight or flight. This is His option: Rest or flight. In this scripture we see that the options were to rest or to flee. And God offers us the same choices. He offers rest. What if instead of fighting we rested? What if instead of running and fleeing from our problems, we rested. I am not talking about being lazy. I am not talking about avoidance. I am not talking about escapism. We rest in the power and strength of the Lord our God, and say, "God, this is hard, but I am standing with You by my side." In doing so we can receive an attitude and feeling of rest. Psalm 112:1 says *"Praise the Lord. Blessed are those who fear the Lord, who find great delight in His commands."*

Ok, time for a pop quiz, hot shot. What is the fourth commandment? Remember the Sabbath and keep it Holy. Sabbath. SON-Bathing. In Psalm 112, the Lord is telling us to praise Him. He calls those who fear the Lord and find great delight in the Sabbath blessed. To honor the Lord, we must honor the Sabbath and keep it holy. Set apart. A day of rest with God.

Psalm 112 goes on to say in verse six, *"Surely, the righteous..."* (Those who follow God's commands) *"…. will never be shaken."* Never. Can you imagine? *"They will be remembered forever. They will have no fear of bad news."*

Ever.

When the next flat tire comes. When an unexpected bill arrives. When the diagnosis is given. When a job is lost. No matter what comes our way, for those who rest in the Lord, if their hearts are steadfast, the Lord says, *"Their hearts are secure, they will have no fear. In the end they look in triumph on their foes."*

We only have one foe in our lives. The Bible is very clear in the New Testament that we do not wrestle against flesh and blood, brothers and sisters, co-workers, friends, or even in-laws. What we wrestle against are the spiritual forces of wickedness. It is the devil himself that we battle. Scripture tells us that if we find our rest in the Lord, we will look on the devil with no fear. The devil will not win the battle. His scheming and planning will not work. In other words, the sky does not fall on those who rest. There may be troubling things happening around us, but the sky will not fall. Those who rest do not live in the spirit of exasperation.

We do not freak out.

When I had that panic attack at 35,000 feet, it wasn't so much "the sky is falling" as much as I thought, "I am falling out of the sky." My response was not due to a fear of flying. It was actually *accumulated stress*. It was not one singular traumatic event that happened to me that caused me to go into panic mode. We have anxiety because of the accumulation of minor things that, if not dealt with, will overtake our spirits and try to wipe us out. That is the devil's plan. At 35,000 feet I was redlining. I was not Sabbathing. Therefore, I could not unpack on a weekly basis all of the stress I had encountered.

Sabbathing offers us the ability to unload our stress every week so it does not build up to a breaking point. Jesus says, *"Come to me all who are weary and heavy laden and I will give you rest."* We can rest in the Lord anytime, but especially on the Sabbath. When we give God our stress, He does not just take it and leave us empty.

He replaces it with something much better. More on that in the next chapter.

NINE

LEAN

GOD NEVER PROMISES that our lives will be devoid of trouble. In fact, Jesus told His disciples, "In this world, you WILL have trouble." Trouble is coming. However, Jesus does promise us that when troubles come, we will not be void of life. We have all experienced trouble. God wants to give us life and hope even in our trouble. It is possible…if we rest in Him.

We have already learned that scientists have determined that humans need 52 days of rest per year in order to function in a healthy and productive manner. I have some more science to share that reveals what God has said all along. I will begin by introducing you to your second brain. In the book, *Rest*, by Alex Soo-Jong and Kim Pang, we are introduced to the term, "default mode network" (DMN). It is a part of the brain of which many are not aware. It is an extremely invaluable part that, in most of us, is not used to its fullest potential. It is the part of the brain that is known better as the resting brain.

When we think about the brain, we are familiar with the parts that control communication, memory, sight, verbalization, problem solving, etc. Scientists, studying the brain, did research by wiring subjects' brains to electrodes while showing them differential equations. I actually took Differential Equations 1 and 2 at the University of Florida. Although my professor, Dr. Varma, was a loving teacher, those difficult equations are the reason I quit engineering and became a pastor. Needless to say, DiffyQ, as we called it, is extremely difficult math!

Ok, back to the scientists. They measured the brain activity as the subjects were trying to solve these complex equations. They also measured their brain activity at a state of rest and relaxation while the subjects simply sat quietly in a chair. Now you would think the brain's activity would be heightened while solving complex mathematical equations and quiet during the period of rest. As it turns out, the brain activity was nearly identical in both scenarios. The resting brain does not actually rest. The DMN turns up when other parts get turned down. The DMN is only utilized in rest. It remains active while we are in a state of rest.

What does this tell us? While we are resting, we are still achieving. When we are seemingly doing nothing, our brains are doing something. In fact, the DMN is that place where greater creativity comes from. It is the place where sound emotional judgment comes from. It is the place where the scientific term "sanity" comes from. It is the place from which our "aha" moments come. We have all experienced this. We try and try to figure something out but we are stuck. We cannot solve the problem. So, we take a break. Or we go to sleep. And when we are no longer thinking of the problem, suddenly the solution becomes clear.

Scientists call this "mind wandering." Mind wandering is when your brain is focused on a mindless task. For example, driving a car. We have done it a million times. The brain slows down a bit because it does not have to work hard to remember how to drive. And suddenly, we have a great idea. This is why we get great ideas in the shower. Because we are in auto mode. Sometimes we get out of the shower and can't remember washing our hair. We know we did, but it was so automatic and habitual that we didn't have to think about it. While the brain is on autopilot, creativity in our brain flourishes. Wise truth comes to mind. Clarity about a solution to a problem is achieved. Scientists call this moment of "Eureka" a particular term. They call it *illumination*.

In order to grow our default mode network, there is one thing we must do. I'll bet you'll never guess. Science tells us that to access the creative power that is in this part of our brain we must rest. Just as God tells us to do.

Rest. This is what God has been telling us from the beginning. He created us and He knows what is best for us. It is part of the DNA He put into us. Yet we do not access this part of our brain because we do not rest. Rest offers us so much. God wants us to have greater emotional judgment. He wants us to be sane. He wants us to have "aha" moments and breakthroughs. But we are trying too hard, in our own power, to do it ourselves. When what we need to do is spend some time SONbathing.

Here is more science that I find fascinating. In school we learned about the nervous system. The Autonomic Nervous System is a fancy way of describing the automatic things that the body does without effort on our part. Breathing and the beating of our hearts are autonomic functions of the body. You might not have been aware of your breathing until I just mentioned it. It happens autonomously.

The Sympathetic Nervous System is the accelerator. It is the area that ignites the fight or flight response. It is the part of our nervous system that tells us, "There is a bear. RUN!!!" or "DEF CON 1." "This is war. FIGHT!" It is an instinctual response to stimuli around us.

The Parasympathetic Nervous System is the brake. It slows us down. It whispers in our ear, "You are safe. It's ok." Sympathetic is anxiety and panic, while parasympathetic is peace. Both are gifts from God. They are both meant to be in us to protect us in certain seasons and situations. But some of us have learned to live in the realm of the sympathetic nervous system. It dictates the way we live, and it leads us to a dangerous redlining place that does not end well. Is your sympathetic switch always on? Are you always bracing, fearing the worst? Are you Chicken Little? Is the sky falling?

My first panic attack was actually not at 35,000 feet, but in a hospital room after my first son was born. It had nothing to do with my son. It had everything to do with hospitals, blood, and needles. I had been accumulating stress because I had a history of passing out around blood. When I was applying for an insurance plan when we were expecting our son, a woman came to our house to draw blood for testing that the insurance company required. Well, she was as good with needles as a two-year-old with a full cup. Disaster awaits. I passed out on my couch. The next time I passed out was during a birthing class. The instructor was giving detailed information about c-sections (GROSS), and I passed out again. So finally, it was time for the birth. About 2:00 in the afternoon, Owen was born. I did fine. Surprisingly. However, at 2:00 in the morning, all I could see in my mind was horrific images of blood. I had a panic attack. It was supposed to be the best night of my life. The birth of my first child. And instead, I could not get off the bed. I ruined it. In that moment I felt like, suddenly, the door to fear had been slung wide open in my life and I could not get it to close. Over the next two years, there were many times when fear would overtake me, and I would just go down. I passed out many times.

You see, before I learned to rest, the door of fear was open, and the sympathetic nervous system switch was set to ON. The dial was fully up. I lived in that place with anxiety and exasperation rushing through me all day long. I could not sit in a movie theater without thinking I was going to pass out. I could barely preach without thinking I was going to pass out.

Finally, after my panic attack at 35,000 feet, when that door to fear was once again pushed open, the Elders of the church helped me. From that point on, when the sympathetic nervous system—that switch—was turned on again, I would send one-word texts to the Elders. The word was LEAN. I pictured the Elders leaning with me against the door of fear to close it so it would be shut. And it was shut. Praise God.

Science has finally figured out what God has known from the beginning. They have learned methods and practices that help us to lean on the door of fear so that it is shut. As you read through the following list, just keep remembering that what scientists are now suggesting is what God has been saying all along. Saying? How about commanding!

Number one is to spend time in nature. We should go to the beach. We should put our toes in the sand and in the water. We should sit and watch the sunrise or the sunset. We should walk through the trees. Go rafting. Whatever we enjoy in nature has a way of resetting our nervous system to a healthy state.

Number two. Practice meditation. Psalm 1, written long before scientists discovered this truth, says, "Blessed is the one who does not walk in step with the wicked, or stand in the way that sinners take, or sit in the company of mockers, but whose delight is in the law of the Lord, and who *meditates* on His law day and night."

Number three is deep, abdominal breathing. When I was going through my struggles I went to a Christian counselor. He said, "All right, we are going to breathe together." It was a bit awkward. But I did it. In the process of breathing together, he observed that I was breathing wrong. Who knew? Forty-plus years old and this guy says I don't know how to breathe? But he told me I was breathing from my chest. He instructed me to expand my stomach, not my chest, when I breathed in. It forces more oxygen in the places that need oxygen. It is the way it is designed. It was given to us by the Lord.

Number four. Repetitive prayer.

Number five. Focus on a word that is soothing. How about THE Word?

Number six. Play with animals or children. Now some of us will not find this restful. But most of us will.

Number seven. Exercise. Can we exercise on the Sabbath? Isn't it work? We can exercise on the Sabbath. It is a work that gives life.

Number eight is progressive relaxation. I highly recommend it. It is simple to do. And it is a gift from God. There are many resources that will teach you how to practice this.

Number nine. Get a hobby. Find something you enjoy doing, something that gives you life, and then do it.

It looks to me that science affirms the Creator's best design for our lives. Rest. Sabbath. And you will find life for your weary soul.

TEN

TRIUMPH ON THE HEIGHTS

THE BEST BOOK on Sabbath was written by a man named Abraham Heschel. Abraham is a Messianic Rabbi who loves Jesus. I believe he wrote the authoritative book on Sabbath. It's called "Sabbath." Nailed the title. If you want to read one book on Sabbath, get this book. He says in his book, "Sabbath is the one day we don't master civilization, we surpass it." Trying to master civilization is trying to invent something to make this life work. To master civilization is to pay all the bills on time, to get the job, get the raise, to exercise and get my bodily temple exactly right. These are certainly good things, but there's one day a week where we surpass civilization because God is above it all.

We join Him.

With God, we are not above it all, better than it all. Rather, we are just not concerned with it all. Not pushing and driving toward the American dream. With God sitting in front of us, we dream of Heavenly places. Uniting with God, we surpass civilization instead of mastering it. Instead of being mastered by civilization and the proverbial "rat race," you can surpass it.

Would you like to guess how?

At this point it's going to feel like I'm piling on, and that's exactly what I'm trying to do. I don't want you to stop reading here wondering whether or not you should be Sabbathing. If you're at the point of, "Dude, we got it," then I'm still going to tell you more.

Isaiah says in chapter 58, verse 14, "Then you will find your joy in the Lord, and I will cause you to ride In triumph on the heights of the land and to feast on the inheritance of your father Jacob." Who wouldn't want that joy? Or to triumph on the heights of the land? Or to feast on the inheritance of Jacob? Note, verse 14 is a "then" statement.

Which means it's a conditional statement. The "if" is found in the preceding verse that, when adhered to, produces the fruit of verse 14. Look at verse 13: " If you keep your feet from breaking the Sabbath and from doing as you please on my Holy day, if you call the Sabbath a delight and the Lord's Holy day honorable, and if you honor it by not going your own way or not doing as you please or speaking idle words, then you will find your joy in the Lord and I will cause you to ride in triumph on the heights of the land and to feast on the inheritance of your father Jacob."

As mentioned before, when we Sabbath we begin to unpack the stuff we've been carrying around. Accumulated stress starts to drain out. As it drains out, the Lord replaces it with His goodness. Specifically in Isaiah 58, we learn of three powerful gifts the Lord gives us in Sabbath rest.

Joy. Triumph on the heights. The inheritance of Jacob.

Anytime we read joy in the Bible it means "grace recognized." Joy is when we stop for a moment and say, "My Lord, You are good. You do good and mighty things in my life even when I don't deserve it. I just want to express my gratitude." Even as I write this, a smile comes to my face because of His goodness and grace. If we desire the joy, joy, joy down in our hearts, we must Sabbath.

We get to Sabbath.

Secondly the Lord said that we would triumph on the heights. If you've ever lost a competition, you know the somber mood that follows. And if you've ever won a competition, you also know the soaring feeling of accomplishment.

Winner, winner, chicken dinner.

When we read "heights" in the Bible, it usually refers to a place of victory or influence, and in this case, it means both because God says triumph on the heights. As we empty out the stress of our lives on a Sabbath, the Lord packs into us influence from a place of victory. When we walk through the earth we're not acting as victims, the outcome of a bad decision or wound. Instead, we have the victorious mentality of our God. He is able. He's done great and mighty things. When we Sabbath, the Lord packs victory into our spirit, chicken dinner indeed. (Although Jesus would have said, "Winner, winner, lamb for dinner.")

Finally, as a result of Sabbath, God is going to give us the inheritance of Jacob. Have you ever read Jacob's will? If not, line one notes that Jacob has left a Ferrari and line two notes he left a house in Colorado. Ok, neither of those is there. There's only one line item on Jacob's will. Only one thing Jacob left behind to his family, and it has been passed now to us.

Blessing.

Instead of stress and curses, we receive blessing. God for us. Not against us. Wind at our backs. When life is hard, we're not void of life. That's blessing. Our material possessions multiplying—that's blessing. Our immaterial possessions, peace, joy, and love multiplying—that's blessing. This is the inheritance that comes from Jacob. This is the inheritance that comes to you when you Sabbath.

Jesus Himself said in Mark chapter 2, verse 27: "The Sabbath was made for man, not man for the Sabbath." It might seem a confusing scripture, but Sabbathing is sowing and reaping. We do not sow into the Kingdom on the Sabbath, the Kingdom sows into us, and then the Kingdom reaps from a rested, blessed us.

My bank account does not help Bill Gates's bank account in the very least. My wealth is not even a drop in the ocean compared to his. Bill Gates has no need of my money. So it is with the Sabbath. There's nothing that we do or bring to the day that helps the Sabbath, but everything about the Sabbath benefits and helps us so that we can be a blessing to the world.

One of my very dearest friends in all the earth lived for fifty years with the sympathetic switch turned on. Fifty years tense and stressed. Chicken Little in the flesh, convinced something bad was going to happen. This meant

;that, in order to maintain sanity, everything had to be in order, homeostasis, everything calm or he could lose it! He lived like this for 50 years because he was raised in the home of an alcoholic father. As you might expect, his father was verbally abusive, which often included the threat of physical abuse. Understandably, this man was living fight or flight every time his dad walked into the house. He had to be prepared to clinch up and fight or to run out of there. This stress became normal to him. Normal. He thought this was just how everyone lived. He was hardwired at a very young age to live from a place of stress.

As I began sharing my story of anxiety and stress and learning this whole Sabbath thing, this man began to introspect his own life. He went to see a counselor. Through this process this man discovered life. He began to learn what the sympathetic and the parasympathetic systems were and how to relax. He began to rest in the grace and goodness of God. For the first time in his life, herealized that the way of living that he'd accepted as normal for all that time wasn't normal at all. There's a place of peace to reside which produces calm and goodness all the days of his life—not just on vacations, but every day. For my friend, the sympathetic switch that was constantly ON is now being flipped off. Rest moves us from the sympathetic system to the parasympathetic. Is your switch stuck on? Follow my friend's path.

Rest.

Start today.

Move forward declaring, "Because my King of Kings has defeated my enemy utterly and completely, I'm riding on the triumph of the heights."

ELEVEN

SABBATH AND SANCTITY

I LOVE WEDDINGS. Weddings are full of beauty and love and hope and promise. My favorite part of every wedding is the moment the officiant (often me) says, "Please rise." Everyone stands as the music swells, and turns to catch their first glimpse of the beautiful bride. I remember when Christine and I got married. The music that was playing was the traditional wedding song. The church had a humongous pipe organ, and the whole room was reverberating with the sound of the music. The doors opened, and there she was. My beautiful bride.

Most everyone has been to weddings. We know that magical moment. It is a special moment in time when everyone turns to face the bride. Right now, think of that moment. Think of how it feels. Think of the great expectation when welcoming the bride into the room. THAT is how we should feel about the Sabbath. Every week God has set aside for us to experience that anticipation and that moment of expectancy and excitement as our twenty-four-hour rest with Him is about to begin. Something great is about to happen.

The Sabbath is a command that should be seen as a gift of life for us. When God created the world, as seen in Genesis 2:3, He created the Sabbath, then He blessed it and set it apart as holy.

Fast-forward hundreds of years and we find ourselves in the book of Exodus. As the book of Exodus begins, we find God's chosen people leaving Egypt after many years of slavery and bondage. These were the people that God chose to bring forth His message. They were not chosen because they were better than all other humans. They were simply the people whom God chose to show His power and majesty, and through whom He would show Himself to the world. They were to represent God to all the nations, showing what it looks like to serve and love the Holy God of the universe so the world could know Him. They were the people to show the world that He offers freedom from bondage, freedom from brokenness. And they were to live holy lives through the Lord by following His commands, which ensured the very outcome He wanted—if obeyed.

In Exodus 20, the Lord gave Moses ten commandments so that the chosen would be a people set apart. In Exodus 20:8, the fourth commandment says, *"Remember the Sabbath day by keeping it holy."* In Genesis, GOD makes the Sabbath holy. Then, in Exodus, He tells the people to remember the day and keep it holy. When we marry the Sabbath, we set this day apart for the Lord, as we set apart a spouse. It is special. It is consecrated. There are many amazing people on the earth, but I am only set apart for my spouse, and my spouse for me.

In Chapter four we discussed Ephesians 5, where the Lord talks about marriage. He says, *"Husbands, love your wives just as Christ loved the church."* He goes on to tell us about Jesus so that husbands will follow His example. *"Jesus gave himself up for her to make her holy, cleansing her by the washing with water through the word, and to present her to himself as a radiant church without stain or wrinkle or any other blemish, but holy and blameless."* Jesus asked husbands to sanctify their wives. To sanctify means to purify. Now, as I said earlier, no man has the power to make his wife holy. Only God can do that. God is simply telling husbands to be like Jesus. For example, when He washed the disciples' feet, Peter asked Jesus if Jesus could wash his whole body and not just his feet. Jesus responded that Peter did not need his whole body to be washed because he'd been saved by faith. He is simply washing Peter's feet, because it is his feet that have been in contact with the world.

So, by sanctifying, we are cleansing ourselves. It is not a return to holiness. We are holy forever solely because of Jesus Christ. When we die and go to heaven, Jesus will see us as holy. Sanctification happens here on earth to cleanse us from any contact that we have had with the world.

The world contacts us on a daily basis. To sanctify someone is to lead them from sin and toward God. When I ask you to marry the Sabbath, I am asking you to take a day that you deliberately and intentionally lead away from sin and toward God. You may say, "Aren't I supposed to do that every day?" The answer is, of course, yes. However, the Sabbath is set apart. Holy.

In our church, my wife and I were in an amazing community group led by some dear friends. We met in their home. The group was made up of a great cross-section of people. My wife and I simply attended this group. We did not lead it, which is awesome! One evening, the group was discussing the difference between every other day and the Sabbath. "If we are supposed to be holy and communing with God every day, then what is different about the Sabbath?"

A few things.

First, on the Sabbath we cease doing everything that we normally do. That is the big deal. We cease working to prove our worth, and instead, we rest in the worth of Jesus. That is a huge difference.

Second, on the Sabbath we consciously lead the day away from sin and toward the Lord. Think of it this way. One of the community group members said she thinks of Sabbath as a birthday. We love our kids every day, but on their birthdays, we do something special. We shower extra attention, praise, and love on them. That's how the Sabbath should be celebrated. There is a direction of our heart and an intention in the way we do things. We are more focused and concentrated on aligning ourselves with God.

That is what it means to Sabbath.

Focus. Intention.

I want to walk us through some Biblical wedding and marriage concepts so that we can embrace the Sabbath differently. This will teach us how to Sabbath while also reinforcing why we need the Sabbath in the first place.

To have a good wedding, we have to first prepare for the wedding.

I made the mistake a while back looking at a certain website. It was bride.com. I don't know if you have ever visited that site before, but it was a dark hole of over-preparation and over-expenditures. If you work for bride.com and you are reading this, I do not mean to offend you. I just mean it scared me. Like hives, lots. Apparently, there are programs and formulas you can follow to ensure one is prepared for the wedding day. There is a twelve-month program that you can follow on this website. This twelve-month program lists 77 steps to wedding day preparation. 77 STEPS!!!! Here are some of the highlights. "12 months out: Determine the budget. Make a guest list. Hire a wedding planner. Decide formality and overall theme. Select a venue. Select a caterer. 11 months out: Choose a color theme and start thinking about the design. Hire vendors who book up quickly, including photographer, band, DJ, and videographer." That's a lot of money right there in that one line. "Ten months out: Start shopping for your wedding dress. Book hotel room blocks for guests. Create your wedding website. Take engagement photos. Begin looking at invitations......nine months out.......eight months out......seven months out.......six months out.....five months out.......four months out: Have your final tasting with the caterer. Choose your cake. Buy wedding bands. Select groomsmen attire and schedule fittings within the month. Hair and make-up trial..............." Yeah, I skipped the hair trial for my wedding.

And it continues. Finally, we get to the week before the wedding. "Manicure and Pedicure. Get a massage. Final dress fitting. Pack your bags for the honeymoon. Clean your ring. Chase down any RSVP stragglers. Deliver the final headcount. Practice your vows out loud. Write your partner a note.........On the night before the wedding: Eat a healthy meal. Pack a clutch." (I had to look up the definition of this word—it is a small bag, if you did not already know, not a part of an engine. Apparently engine parts are not needed for weddings.) And the list goes on and on.

Seventy-seven steps of preparation for one singular day. I could be wrong, but that seems a little excessive to me. Maybe it seems reasonable to you. Maybe you know or were a bridezilla. That's great! There is no right or wrong way to prepare for a wedding. My point is not to say that this type of preparation is wrong. My point is that the wedding preparation affects the wedding experience. It takes so much pre-planning and preparation to make the day special. So it is with the Sabbath. Our Sabbath day and its effectiveness completely hinges on our Sabbath preparedness. How we prepare for the Sabbath determines how our Sabbath goes. (However, sometimes the Lord just gives grace, and it's amazing even when we do nothing to prepare.)

The Israelites' account in Exodus is a story that shows how the people over and over made mistakes. They did not trust God. They did not obey God. God was constantly revealing Himself to them, calling them to obedience, devotion, and worship. He promised them that He would be their God and provide for them if they worshipped Him and followed His laws. But they still grumbled and complained. Because of their unfaithfulness to God, they wandered in the wilderness for forty years before they finally entered the promised land.

In Exodus 16, we read of God's daily provision of food for His people while they were in the wilderness. It was called "manna." The word "manna" simply means, "What is it?" Sounds like something my family would say when I cook. I digress. For forty years the Israelites woke up in the morning and would gather enough manna for their household for one day. Exodus 16:21 says, *"Each morning everyone gathered as much as they needed and when the sun grew hot, it melted away. On the sixth day, they gathered twice as much, two omers, (that's a unit of measurement) for each person."* Moses told them that the Lord commanded that the seventh day was to be a day of rest—a holy Sabbath to the Lord. So, on the sixth day, the Israelites were told to collect twice as much, then bake and boil and save half for the next day, the Sabbath. Verse 24 says, *"So they saved it until the morning as Moses commanded and it did not stink or get maggots in it."* On the other days of the week, manna was spoiled if it was saved for the next day. However, on the Sabbath day, there was no manna on the ground to gather, so God miraculously preserved the manna that they gathered on the sixth day to be carried over to the next day. They had to be prepared. The Lord instructed them to prepare for the Sabbath day by taking a double portion the day before. If the preparation was not there, the provision was not there. If the preparation wasn't there, the provision wasn't there. Yes, I wrote it twice on purpose.

TWELVE

DIRTY DISHES

MY WIFE AND I used to practice Sabbath on Mondays. The kids would get home from school, and we would practice Sabbath with our kids in the afternoon until bedtime. So, instead of a 24-hour Sabbath, the whole family was only actually getting four to six hours. We realized that we were doing a disservice to our children and to God.

We decided to make a change and practice the Sabbath on Friday evening, beginning at 5:30 dinner and ending at 5:30 dinner on Saturday. It disrupted our normal rhythm pretty significantly. We used to do all our chores on Saturday. We would wake up, get the laundry going, get our rooms cleaned, and clean the rest of the house. We realized that we were using our day off from work and school to clean and do housework. Now we do things differently. I try to make sure that by Friday at 5:30PM the laundry is done. (I do all the laundry in our house and my wife does all the grocery shopping—cool beans, huh?) By Friday at 5:30 pm, all of us have done our chores (ideally, although it doesn't always work out in reality). The kids clean their rooms, the bathrooms are cleaned, and meal prep is done, all so that on Friday evening we do not have to work. We prepare for the Sabbath.

My wife even decorates our dinner table beautifully beforehand. When we get home on Friday afternoons, we know that something special is about to happen. The house smells good. The house looks good. We all scramble around a little bit during the last few minutes before 5:30, but then 5:30 arrives. We sit down. We have the Shabbat meal, or the Sabbath dinner, which begins with prayer. We light candles. We welcome the Sabbath. I walk around the table with a towel around my shoulders. It was originally an orange towel with polka dots. I know that sounds kind of strange, but now I wear a stole (a long scarf worn by clergy). The stole represents priestly authority and covering. As the head of my household, I wear the stole to represent covering my family in the presence of the Lord. We ceremonially wash our hands with a warm, wet towel and we begin eating. We pray a blessing over the bread.

Candles represent His presence. The cleansing of hands represents His purity applied to us. The bread is His provision. Presence. Purity. Provision. This is how we start our Sabbath. We eat our meal, then I lay the stole on top of each of my children and pray a blessing on each of them. Then the children and I go to my wife and, together, pray a blessing on her. And guess what we do after dinner?

We leave the dishes in the sink for the entire Sabbath.

Does the thought of that freak anyone out? "You can't leave dirty dishes in the sink." But we do. They stay there until the 24-hour period ends. Then we put them in the dishwasher. Now, these things I have listed are just what my family does. It is not a legalistic rule. Every family must decide for themselves what Sabbath looks like for them. All of us must listen to the Holy Spirit and do what He tells us to prepare for and observe the Sabbath.

When we prepare for and honor the Sabbath in this way, it is amazing how peaceful and enjoyable the following 24 hours are. Normally, in the Ingram family, there is a flare-up here and there. People are annoyed and arguing and weeping and gnashing their teeth. You know, human stuff. But when we Sabbath, there is a peace and calm that come over us. We are free.

The second thing we need to begin the Sabbath is to welcome the bride. In the Jewish custom, there is a song that is 400 years old. In Hebrew, the title means, "Come my beloved." They sing it either at the temple service together to begin a Sabbath, or they sing it in their own homes. It is usually a very upbeat song. And during the very last chorus, everybody stands and faces the door. It is very cool. Look it up on YouTube if you want to see for yourself.

The whole congregation stands up and faces the door, just like people in a wedding anticipating seeing the bride. In their heart of hearts, as they stand and turn, the people are welcoming the Sabbath. For Messianic Jews—Jews that believe in Jesus—they turn to the door and say, "Jesus, this is your day. Come on in. Please come in and share this day with us!" Great perspective to start a Sabbath!

I am now going to share with you the lyrics to this song (Lecha Dodi) that the Jewish people use to welcome God.

Come my beloved to meet the bride,
And let us welcome Shabbat.

"Safeguard" and "Remember" singly uttered,

So we heard it from the singular one.
God is one and God's name is one
reflected in fame and splendor and praise.

To greet Shabbat let's go, let's travel,
For she is the wellspring of blessing,
From the start, from ancient times chosen,
Last made, but first planned.

Sanctuary of the king, royal city,
Arise! Leave from the midst of turmoil;
Long enough have you sat in the valley of tears
He will take great compassion pity on you

Shake yourself free, rise from the dust,
Dress in your garments of splendor,
By the hand of Jesse's son of Bethlehem,
Redemption draws near to my soul.

Come, rouse yourself! Rouse yourselves!
Your light is coming, rise up and shine.
Awaken! Awaken! Utter a song,
The glory of the Lord is revealed upon you.
Do not be embarrassed! Do not be ashamed!
Why be downcast? Why do you moan?
All my afflicted people will find refuge within you
And the city shall be rebuilt as in ancient days.

Your despoilers shall be your spoil.
Far away shall be any who would devour you,
Your God will rejoice concerning you,
As a groom rejoices over a bride.

To your right and your left you will burst forth,
And the Lord will you revere
By the hand of a child of Peretz,
We will rejoice and sing happily

(Stand and turn before final stanza)
Come in peace, crown of her husband,
Both in happiness and in jubilation
Amidst the faithful of the treasured nation
Come O Bride! Come O Bride!

No matter how you practice your Sabbath, I pray that you will practice this part. Or at some moment, as you begin, you stop and either physically, or simply in your heart, stand up and face the door and say, "Welcome." When my family lights candles, the light is a representation of the Lord's coming into our presence. His manifest presence. He is there with us. We welcome the bride.

Third, after we prepare for the Sabbath and welcome the bride, we put a ring on it!

When I officiate weddings, I get to the portion where the bride and groom exchange rings and say, "The ring is an unbroken circle of love. It is a representation of the covenant of God's love. It makes the two one in unity." It sounds nice. It is poetic. Blah, blah, blah. But what does the ring really mean? It is a symbol of unity and commitment. A symbol of covenant, surely, but if you are married, I hope that when you see your ring, it reminds you of something more. Do you remember what you felt on your wedding day? The beauty of the place and the people? The joy and expectation in your heart? The surrounding of love from God and every witness to your special day? Every time your ring hits something, and your attention is drawn to it, I hope it is a reminder of the initial glory of that day when two became one. The ring is a reminder of past glory.

The ring is also a reminder of future glory. There are many things in this life that will come and go. Our clothes even daily come and go, but the ring stays on. May it be to you that every time you see your ring, you remember your commitment that, come what may, you will be faithful until parted by death.

The ring also declares something to the rest of the world. Single ladies, when a good-looking man walks into the room, and his hands are in his pocket, do you hope that he is single? When his left hand comes out of his pocket and you see a ring, it tells you to move on—he's off the market, so to speak. The wedding ring tells the rest of the world, "I am taken. I belong to another."

The Sabbath also says to the devil, "I'm taken." The Bible tells us that the devil is prowling about like a lion, seeking to devour us. Every day and every night, the enemy is plotting and scheming against us. The Bible says, "The accuser stands before the Lord, day and night." The enemy seeks to accuse and destroy us. But when we practice the Sabbath, we show the devil that we are "taken" by Jesus, causing the devil to give up and move on.

Exodus 31:12 says, "Then the Lord said to Moses, 'Say to the Israelites, you must observe the Sabbath. This will be a sign [a ring] between me and you for the generations to come, so you may know that I am the Lord who makes you holy." When we practice Sabbath, it reminds us of our salvation.

Psalm 51:12 says, "Restore unto me the joy of my salvation." God, remind me what it was like the day that I bent my knee to you and said, "Yes, Father. Forgive me of my sins. Receive me into Your glory forever and ever. Fill me with that joy." The Sabbath will remind us of the past glory, the initial glory, and the joy of the day that we were saved. It will also remind us of future glory. Every time we Sabbath, we dip our toes into the grandeur of Heaven. We get a little taste.

I Corinthians 13 tells us that we see but in a poor reflection. It is kind of dim. Have you ever gotten in the car early in the morning and everything is coated in water and your view of the road is clouded? That is how we see the future glory of Heaven during Sabbath. But one day we will see face to face the glory of God. The grandeur of God. Every time we Sabbath, we get a little picture of what Heaven is like. In Heaven, we will not work but will be resting in Him and worshipping Him forever.

THIRTEEN

MORE THAN CRUMBS

HERE IS THE ISSUE. Some of us have been saved for a great portion of our lives. Some of us have never been saved. And both groups of people believe the same thing: They are nothing and worth nothing. It is true. The Bible is pretty clear that before we received Jesus, we were like a filthy pile of rags. So indeed, we are nothing apart from Christ Jesus. That is not condemnation. It is simply a condition of sin. We have fallen short of the glory of God, and, therefore, we are broken and dead in our sins. We are dead in our transgressions. I lived there for a long portion of my life before I was saved.

Because we have sinned, we think less of ourselves. We think we are not worthy of the love and rest of Jesus.

But what if we were wrong? Let me explain.

Before I go on, let me just note this is the fourth part of the Sabbath. First, preparation. Second, welcoming the Bride. Third, putting a Ring on It. And fourth and finally, the two become one on the Sabbath. In marriage, the two become one and identity changes for both. The individuals no longer are individual persons, but they are now a couple. The "me" becomes a "we." The two become one. So it is with the Sabbath. Our identity is transformed.

How many of you who are married have ever been told, "Wow! You married up!"? We all know what it means. This is what we do as humans. We look and inspect physically and practically. We check the outside and we check the inside of a person. Then we make a judgment. We judge the book by its cover, and then we read the book. So, by the outflow of life and by the appearance of a person, we may say, "Wow, she's a 10." And then we look over at her husband, make the same determinations and say, "Whoa, he's only a 6. He married up."

I want to declare that this line of thinking is nonsense. Would an actual ten choose anything other than a ten? If she is indeed a ten, she took all of her ten-ness, all of her wisdom, all of her grace, all of her beauty, all of her poise, everything that the Lord has given her, and she also chose a ten. A ten would not choose a six. A ten only chooses a ten. Otherwise, a ten is not a ten. In that case the ten may actually be a two who made a bad mistake. Are you following? She did not choose a six out of pity. She chose a ten because he is a ten. This is an identity issue. An identity crisis.

When we receive Jesus through faith, we are no longer a one, or a two, or a three, four, five, six, seven, eight, or nine. We are either a zero or a ten because of the name of Jesus. Every time that we Sabbath, the perfect ten (Jesus) walks in the door and says, "Hello, ten. Good to see you, ten. I'm glad to have dinner with you, ten." We may feel like a three. But Jesus sees us as a ten. Jesus (a ten) chose another ten, you.

Recently, I had a conversation with a dear friend of mine. He was living overseas, and we were communicating on WhatsApp. We were basically texting internationally. The Lord put him on my heart, so I texted him. He responded and said, "Hey man, you were also on my heart, and I began praying for you." He had written out what he prayed and shared it with me.

He said, "I believe that when people are suddenly thrust on my heart it is for a reason. So, I usually start praying. Rarely do I get visions, though. But when I have, they have been life-changing. I don't want to blow this off. I was praying for loved ones the other night, and you....[that's me]....suddenly came to the forefront of my mind. So, I focused my mind, heart, and soul on you in prayer. Several minutes later, as I'm praying, I come to realize that I'm watching a man on his knees bent over with his face near the ground."

He continued, "I was curious. I got down close to see what this man was doing down there. I put my face right next to his and saw he was an older gentleman. I saw what looked like a rectangular cracker or cookie on the ground before him and it was crumbling before his eyes. He was picking up small morsels and eating them. Crumbs really. At that point, I wondered who he was and where we were. I looked down and the ground was a very old marble or stone with a pattern to it. Maybe three colors. I looked up and around and, in all directions, as far as I could see, the flooring went on and on and on. We were alone and seemingly nowhere. At this point, I realized I was still praying for you and as if out of a fog or haze, I came to realize that I was having a vision. I can still see it all like it was just a second ago. But honestly, I have no idea if it was for you or for me?"

After I read this text, I immediately felt I knew what it was about. The vision was clear to me, so I responded to my friend. "Eating crumbs when we have been invited to the table." That was what I heard and understood from his vision. God was saying, "I have so much more for you, my son. Choose it now, or in 30 years you will still be a crumb eater."

However, I was not sure what to make of the three colors. Later, when I was sharing this with my staff, one of our pastors said, "The three colors represent the triune God, and the pattern on the floor is the fact that you are in the royal palace, and yet you are on the floor of the palace instead of sitting at the table."

The unending pattern of the floor gave me the sense of a timeless trap, being a crumb eater. It was an identity crisis. Crumb eaters live daily feeling unworthy. Crumb eaters feel undeserving, which, apart from Jesus, I was. But now, as a son of the King through faith in Jesus, I am so deserving, not because of anything I have done, but because of whose name I bear. The enemy bows at the name of Jesus. Provision jumps off trees into my hand at the name of Jesus.

Darkness flees at the name of Jesus. I told my friend that I wasn't sure if the vision is solely for me or for both of us. (Nebuchadnezzar, who was a king in the Bible, had a vision and brought it to Daniel, and Daniel interpreted the dream for Nebuchadnezzar.) My friend answered, "You could have dreamed a dream in relation to me as I was to be the interpreter God wanted you to bring the vision to. No matter, we both need to live as sons and not as beggars."

Right after I read that text, I went to do my morning reading. I came across a particular passage of Scripture, and I texted him back, "So you said you had been feeling things, and then you ran into verses—Scripture that is spot on to what you were feeling." Yes, that is what he had told me. I continued, "Well, I just read Galatians 4:4-7, which says, *"But when the set time had fully come, God sent His son, born of a woman, born under the law, to redeem those under the law that we might receive adoption to sonship or daughtership because you are His sons and daughters. God sent the spirit of His son, Jesus, into our hearts, the spirit who calls out Abba, Father. So you are no longer a slave."* No longer a crumb eater. *"But God's child. And since you are His child, God has also made you an heir."*

I sent the first text at 6:10 am and at 6:17 am that morning I was reading that verse. Seven minutes later. To me the number seven always sticks out as the number of perfection. God was aligning things that my friend and I could understand. He was calling both of us to not be on the floor begging for crumbs from the Savior when we are heirs to the throne and invited to the table.

The Lord says in Psalm 23, "I prepare a table for you in the presence of your enemies." The Sabbath is a table. It has been set for us. The Lord invites us to come each and every week to sit down. We do not have to beg at His feet. We get to sit at the table as sons and daughters with the inheritance of the Lord our God coming our way. It is a promise to all who believe. The promise is received as we Sabbath.

FOURTEEN

LESS IS MORE

MY GOAL FOR this book is for us to unlearn the way we rest and, instead, learn to rest like God rests, so that our rest becomes His rest and, better yet, His rest becomes our rest. His rest is restorative in all its ways.

I still find it amazing that God wants us to rest. In fact, He doesn't just want us to rest. For our sake, He commands us to rest. To Sabbath. The Sabbath is a holy and sacred rest. Twenty-four hours set aside for God. To rest as God commands us is to celebrate. We rest and enjoy. We rest and renew in the rest of God.

Even though we are nearing the end of this book, our learning about the Sabbath will go on and on. This is why we practice the Sabbath. Every week, when we rest as God has instructed us to do, we are practicing. We are continuing to intentionally hear from the Lord.

People often ask me how to Sabbath. What exactly should we do? Before I answer that question, know that none of us will be able to perfect the Sabbath here on earth. That will not happen until we are in Heaven. Let's give ourselves some grace and enjoy the journey.

So, what exactly do we do? How does one Sabbath? What should I do? What should I not do? There is one simple answer to these questions: Ask the Holy Spirit to guide you.

Now that may seem like a cop-out, but it is not. The only way to know what our individual Sabbath should look like is if we each ask the Holy Spirit to teach us and lead us throughout the day. Jesus said that the Holy Spirit would be our teacher. Therefore, Holy Spirit should be the one who teaches us how to Sabbath. Our relationship with the Holy Spirit is one of love. The Sabbath is not just a box to check off on our to-do list. The Holy Spirit wants us to ask and plan how to interact with God. In the same way you plan an outing with people you love, so take the time with Holy Spirit and plan out your Sabbath.

We can even plan ahead! We could dream of ways we can celebrate Sabbath in the future. Maybe it is a special day trip. Maybe it is a hike in nature. Maybe it is a day at the beach. Maybe it is a day of rest and relaxation and an epic nap (Yes, Lord!!!) We could be planning all week long. We can plan months ahead. The Sabbath is supposed to be something we enjoy and look forward to, like a much-needed vacation. The Holy Spirit will lead us in ways to find this refreshment, celebration, and rest!

Before I continue, I want to say that, in this book, I have barely scratched the surface on the subject of Sabbath. I am simply sharing what God has taught me and has laid on my heart to share with others. There are many other books and resources that teach more about this amazing command and gift from God to us. I would like to share two recommendations of books that I have read and learned from. I pray they will help you along, as well.

The first book is called *The Rest of God* by Mark Buchanan. The second book is called *Sabbath* by Abraham Herschel, which I mentioned previously. Some of you out there are researchers and desire to understand more about this great command to rest. This is certainly not a comprehensive list of all truth about the Sabbath, but it is a very good start if you would like to learn more and dive deeper.

The last principle I would like to share about the Sabbath over the next chapters is the principle of More with Less. It is one of those upside-down concepts. If we want more of what God has in store for us, we have to start with what appears to be less. When we live the less way, we get more joy, more discernment, more energy, more faith, more power, more peace.

The Lord put this phrase on my heart: counter-intuitive living. Intuition is our default thinking. Counter refers to the opposite. So counter-intuitive living is thinking and living in a way opposite to what we would normally do. It is living, instead, the way God calls us to live. Watch how God does more with less all throughout the Scriptures.

We read of a man named Paul. He was a church planter. He was an apostle. He wrote a letter to one of the churches that he founded in a city called Corinth. We can read this letter in 1 Corinthians. In 1 Corinthians 1:26, Paul talks about counter-intuitive living. We read, *"Brothers and sisters, think of what you were when you were called."* Let's pause here.

The church in Corinth was receiving this letter, but God meant this letter to exist for all churches for all time. Paul is actually also speaking to us and not just to the church of Corinth. Paul is asking us to think of who we were before Jesus Christ called us into His family. Who we were before Jesus saved us and called us into ministry. Now, that does not necessarily mean that He calls us to stand on a stage and preach. But we are all called to be disciples and lead other people to Christ.

Who were we before Jesus? If we are honest with ourselves, and we look back on our lives before Christ, it's not pretty. We lived for our flesh instead of for God. Think of that for a second. Maybe we were foolish. Maybe we were thieves. Maybe we were selfish. Thankfully, we serve a God who chooses, as Paul goes on to note, "*the foolish things of the world to shame the wise. He chooses the weak things of the world to shame the strong. He chooses the lowly things of the world and the despised things, and the things that are not, to nullify the things that are, so no one may boast before Him.*"

I do not approach God and say, "God, look what I did. I'm amazing." None of us get to God on our own merit. Verses 30 and 31, "*It is because of Him, God, that we are in Christ Jesus who has become for us the wisdom from God. That is our righteousness, holiness, and redemption. Therefore, as it is written, let the one who boasts, boast in the Lord.*"

The Lord our God took a murdering stutterer and asked him to lead two million Israelites on the greatest escape route ever taken. From the hand of Pharaoh and his mighty army, the greatest army in the world at that time, they escaped. Not only did they escape from them, but on the same day, in one single, great move, the Lord God crushed all of Pharaoh and his armies at the gesture of this murdering stutterer. He took the foolish one, Moses, and shamed the wise one, Pharaoh. Well, that's counter-intuitive.

Likewise, God took the weakest person in the weakest family in the weakest clan, and took his army of 30,000 and dwindled it down to 300 people. Those 300 people defeated the mighty Midianite army. Gideon was the leader of that army. Through Gideon, the weak, God shamed the strong Midianites. Counter-intuitive.

In the book of Esther, we see God take a lowly slave girl and make her the queen of a nation. She saved her people from execution. Who was she to do that? She was not of noble birth, but the Lord put her in a high place so that she could influence human history, saving her people from death to life. Counter-intuitive, again!

God took a baby boy, raised to the age of 33, and crucified Him on a cross. And through this death, He brought victory. His name was Jesus. What? He was dead.

How does that bring victory? The people wanted a warrior. But instead, God sent a baby who happened to be the King of Kings. Are you getting the point?

And here is something I find amazing. He took a military brat who was a hypocritical, religious teenager, a lost and confused college student, and he put him in a place to build a church. [That's me]. A church which the gates of hell cannot withstand. It certainly doesn't make sense to me. But I'm not God (aren't you glad about that?)

This is the counter-intuitive Kingdom right in front of our eyes. It is counter-intuitive to us when God takes a vessel, such as you or I, and He does something that does not seem humanly possible. CORRECT! Humanly, it is not possible, but with God, what was impossible suddenly becomes possible—when the fool confounds the wise, when the weak confounds the strong, when God does more with less.

All of this is pretty incredible. Most of us depend on our common sense in life. If we do this, common-sensible things will happen. But I want to suggest to you that as people of God, we should not depend solely on common sense. We want uncommon sense. We want supernatural sense. When we live out what seems to the world to be counter-intuitive, we receive the wisdom of God. When God asks us to give Him one day a week, isn't that counter-intuitive? Couldn't you be more productive with that day? Indeed, it is counter-intuitive, which means it seems very likely to be a Kingdom thing. Believe it!

FIFTEEN

SABBATH AND MONEY

AN EXAMPLE OF counter-intuitive action is tithing. To the world, this principle makes no sense. But I know when I counter-intuitively give God ten percent of my income, my provision, my security, God blesses it and stretches it further than it would have gone. I have more by having less. I have more by giving more.

Do you love tithing stories? Do you love how God does miracles in our lives when we obey? It is a beautiful thing. Well, here's mine. When I was twenty-five years old,

I was working at a church. I made $22,475 per year. LOADED. I was married to my beautiful and wise wife, Christine. She truly is my helpmate. She is a channel of the Holy Spirit in my life. At that point in my life, I confess that I was not tithing. I was, instead, tipping God. I would give Him whatever leftovers I had when I had had a good week. Maybe it was five dollars, maybe it was more. Yup. That was how I was operating. God, you did good this week; here's your tip.

Christine, in all her wisdom, told me one day that we needed to start tithing. I argued with her that we did not make enough money. I did not think we could afford it. She had a physical therapy degree from the University of Florida, but because of so few jobs available, she did not have a full-time job at that time. She worked what I can loosely call part-time because shifts were only available on an as-needed basis. My excuse was that we could not afford to tithe because we did not have enough regular income. Makes sense, right?

Now, what comes next is my story. Please do not do exactly what I did unless the Holy Spirit leads you. The Lord started speaking to my heart through the Holy Spirit and through my wife. The Lord said to us, "Do not pay your rent this month. Give the tithe, and watch what happens." You see, that was our choice, tithe or pay rent.

We only had enough money to allow one or the other, according to human math. The logical person would have paid rent. But, following God's clear instruction, we counter-intuitively tithed instead. We wrote the tithe check, put it in the offering and then tried not to panic but to trust God.

We did not tell anyone what we were doing. On the very next day, my wife received a full-time job offer. That same day she received a second full-time job offer. Say what?? Two days later our landlord called us. They had no idea what was going on in our hearts or in our lives. But our landlord said to me, "Tim, the Lord told us to tell you not to pay your rent this month." Jaw on floor. Hands in air. Praise going up.

Now I'm not a believer in the prosperity gospel which says that we give in order to get. But I am a believer in a provision gospel, which says that as we place our faith and hope and trust in Jesus, and we display that faith by tithing, the Lord is faithful to provide for us. He provides on His terms according to His will, whatever He chooses to provide. The blessing wasn't the financial outcomes. The blessing was what God cemented in our hearts in that four-day span. "You can trust me at my Word, Tim and Christine." And we have ever since.

The Lord doesn't look at money when we give it. He looks at our heart. He is moved by our godly motives. He is moved by our faith in action. Faith is the currency of heaven. Faith moves the heart of God.

This same principle applies to the Sabbath. When we give in faith, He responds to our heart. Both tithing and Sabbathing come down to one question. Who is Lord of all in our lives? If I am lord of my own life, then I am going to put my faith in me to provide everything that I need. The time, the money, the stuff, the rest will all be in my control. But if God is truly the Lord of all in my life, then I am going to trust Him and display it through my actions. I will show that I trust Him and put my faith in Him. And I believe that by giving God one day per week of my time, adoration, and focus, He will bless and make more fruitful the remaining six days.

Psalm 24:1 says, "The earth is the Lord's, and everything in it, the world and all who live in it." Humans, raccoons, worms, fish, and even cockroaches. All of it belongs to the Lord. There are many verses in the Bible that can be hard to understand. In Luke 14:26, for example, Jesus says, "If you do not hate your father, mother, wife, and children, brother and sister, you can't be my disciple." What does that mean? We could have a theology class on this verse. It is difficult to understand. But Psalm 24:1 is not one of those difficult-to-understand verses. It is pretty evident what the Lord is saying. Everything belongs to God. There is nothing that we can think of that does not belong to God.

Knowing that in our spirit, let's look at Leviticus 27:30. "A tithe of everything from the land, whether grain from the soil, or fruit from the trees belongs to the Lord. It is Holy to the Lord." Leviticus 27:30 is saying that a tithe literally means ten percent. Tithe, the ten percent, comes to the Lord. It comes to the storehouse, which is the local church.

Every week I take a check and put it in the little black offering box at the back of the church. Every week I read what is on the top of this box. It says, "Give." And every week I think that is not the right word, because when we bring the tithe to the storehouse, we are not giving it. We are returning to God what already belongs to Him. It is holy to the Lord, set apart for Him.

So, when I drop my check in there every week, I am returning it to the Lord by faith because of what God promises. I trust Him. I have even thought about changing the wording on the offering box, but I think it would confuse people. People might think they are supposed to place their Walmart returns in there. We leave the word "Give" on the box. But I think I am making my point clear.

In Genesis 2:3, we read, *"Then God blessed the seventh day and made it Holy."* He set it apart. It belongs to Him. It is His. It is consecrated because, on it, He rested from all the work of creation He had done.

If we want to unwrap the gift of time, we need to return that time to God by faith. So whatever 24 hours of time that we choose, we take it to the Lord and say, "God, I am returning this time to you. You gave it to me to see what I would do with it and now I am trusting you. You are enough. You have created all things, and You have given life and have sustained life through the blood of Jesus Christ. I am giving this day by faith. I am returning it back to you." When we do this, just like with tithing, we start experiencing miracles in our lives. We do our work by giving the day back to God, and then God does what only He can do.

You see, there was a beginning. God created everything in the first chapter of Genesis. In chapter one He created human beings, and in chapter two, He gave them some instructions. Part of that instruction to Adam and Eve was that they could eat from the Tree of Life. They could live in the garden forever. In the cool of the evening, they could walk with God. They could be naked and have no shame because there was no sin, shame, or condemnation. They were also instructed not to eat of the Tree of the Knowledge of Good and Evil. For their own sakes, God gave this instruction. He knew the destruction that it would bring if it was eaten. He desired to be the Lord God, the one with knowledge of good and evil. He wanted us to leave that to Him. Depend on Him.

But the devil showed up in the form of a serpent. At this point, the serpent was not yet cursed on his belly, so he was probably upright. He asked Adam and Eve, "Did God really say not to eat of that tree? Who is He? I think you should be able to eat the fruit and be like Him. Why don't you eat from that trec, and you will be like God. It will be amazing." Eve saw that it did look pleasing to the eye, so she took the fruit and ate it. Then she gave it to Adam. And Adam ate it, too. After they ate it, they immediately experienced shame. They felt condemnation and they clothed themselves with fig leaves and then hid from God. As a result of this first sin in human history, God declared that because they had acted against God, they invited sin into the world. The consequences were terrible. Humans were removed from the blessing that God had lovingly intended and were turned over to the curse.

He gave woman the curse of painful childbearing. Sorry about that one, ladies. And in Genesis 3:17, He told the man, "Because you listened to your wife and ate from the tree about which I commanded you, 'Do not eat from it,' the ground is cursed because of you. You will eat from it by means of painful labor all the days of your life." By painful labor we now eat. Painful labor will feed our bodies from a cursed land. And this is true for us today.

We work hard all week long. Some of us actually work the ground so that we can feed our bodies by that work. We work hard so we can have a car, so that we do not wear out our bodies by walking everywhere. We work to put gasoline in our cars. We work hard so we can have air conditioning in our homes, so that we can sleep better, so our bodies will function better. We work hard so that we can afford a gym membership so we can work our bodies even harder. (That's weird).

We do so much work to provide for ourselves, our families, and even our bodies. Exodus 20:8 tells us to remember the Sabbath day by keeping it Holy. Six days we should labor. For six days we toil to provide for our bodies and do all our work. But the seventh day is the Sabbath to the Lord our God. God wants us to work hard for the six days, but on the seventh day He wants us to do no work so that He can do His work in our lives.

Study.

Rest.

Pray.

Enjoy.

Celebrate.

Renew.

Resting labor will feed our souls from heaven.

There are two types of labor. One is the toilsome labor that provides for our bodies from a cursed earth. The second is a resting labor that provides for our souls from a blessed heaven. This labor is done through a step of faith that God will provide for us when we trust Him. What does He provide? Read on!

SIXTEEN

COVETOUS VS. CONTENTED

THE SABBATH'S PRODUCTION is reduction. The first thing the Sabbath reduces in us is pride. God reduces our pride when we Sabbath. Pride is the original sin. It is what got Adam and Eve in trouble. They wanted to be like God. They wanted to do things their way. They thought they knew better than the Supreme being of all the universe. Pride is the driving force before and behind all sin. We believe that we know best. We do what we want. We often do not Sabbath because of our pride. We think we know better. Or, we think that we have to keep working so that people will not see us as lazy. We care too much about appearances and achievements. We want praise and adoration from others as a result of the work we do. The things we achieve. The material wealth we display. The outcomes we produce. Nice house! Nice yard! What a car!!

Don't get me wrong. God does not want us to be lazy. He wants us to work hard, as unto Him. He asks us to be productive for six days of the week. But on the Sabbath day, we are to lay it all down at His feet: our work, our busyness, and our pride. Sabbath is a lifestyle that depends on His strength, not our own. We don't depend on ourselves, but on Jesus.

I know a man in the Orlando area who owned two huge construction projects. One was at the Gaylord Palms Resort, and the other was in the Icon Park development. If you live in Orlando, it's where the giant Ferris wheel is located. Together, these projects cost close to 180 million dollars. There were over 300 people working on these job sites. And you'd better believe that in the construction industry, pride is involved. Big egos and big wallets. Meeting deadlines early, saving costs, etc. There is a desire for excellent achievement and recognition of a job well done. Because of this, workers in this industry are willing to work seven days a week to get the approval of superiors. Job sites are always open.

My friend did things differently, though. He is a member of my church family. After learning about the Sabbath in a series of messages that I preached at church, one night in our community group, he told us that he was going to close his job site on Sundays. I was sure that was not going to go over well. Because of all the pride, money, and egos of the many workers involved, striving to get things done well and fast, erecting the Taj Mahal of hotels and beautiful restaurants, it was risky.

But he did it. He shut the job sites down on Sundays. He took a stand for the Lord. He knew in order to Sabbath, he had to close the sites so he would not be tempted to work. And here is what happened.

Personally and professionally, he has been blessed.

All of his bosses flew down on a private plane. These are the people who own the Opryland, Texas, and Palms Gaylords. They flew in to inspect the work. According to my friend, the meeting could not have gone better. He claimed it was one of the best meetings they had ever had. The bosses loved everything that was happening and were pleased that the project was ahead of schedule AND underbudget.

I wonder how that happened.

Can you imagine the conversations around the dinner table of his bosses and co-workers? "Why is the worksite closed on Sundays?" "Some crazy Christian!" My friend put his pride on the line and God honored that step of faith and obedience. He was being protected while great things were happening all around him.

One last nugget from this story before we move on. One day, my friend was flying home from another business trip, this time Nashville, Tennessee. He missed his family and began to write a list of all the things he wished he had time to do with his kids but wasn't doing. Teach them to play baseball. Teach them how to play the banjo (this is his list, not mine!). Build an obstacle course for monster trucks. None of these things did he have time to do. That is, until he started to practice the Sabbath. My friend was obedient to God, and God blessed him personally. His Sabbath days are restful, with no work emails coming to steal his attention and focus from the Lord. He has peace and quiet in his life that he never had when he was working seven days a week. He is proving to be an example to his family and all those around him. This paragraph alone is going to change someone's heart regarding the Sabbath. God wants to give you time with your kids. He commands it!

The Sabbath reduces our pride and increases our dependence on God.

Second, the Sabbath reduces coveting. It reduces coveting and increases contentment. Contentment is the opposite of coveting. We often do not Sabbath because we do not know how to sit in a place and just be content. We worry because everything is not finished. There is more to be done. We feel guilty and lazy. We don't have everything figured out. We worry about finances. But on Sabbath we are asked to be content in the sovereignty of God.

I do not necessarily do a great job of just being still. But what happens when we as the body of Christ begin to practice and to live that? God instructs us to *"Be still and know that I am God."* (Psalm 46:10) When we Sabbath, we are a rock-solid picture of peace. Then, when an emergency hits a few days later, we are still a rock-solid picture of peace because we have trained for these moments during our rest on the Sabbath. We practice contentment, come what may. We rest in the sovereignty and power of the Mighty God, and we are not moved.

Contentedness with God, saying God is enough, helps us to not covet what someone else has or is doing. We don't compare ourselves with others and then drive ourselves to doing more, producing more, running after things of this world. The Lord tells us that He has given us everything we need in the Sabbath. We can say and believe that everything is ok, not because of what we have, but because of who God is. We have all that we need because of what we know about our Savior and His character. We rest assured that God will provide because we are His children. We are His.

Finally, Sabbath reduces fear. Often, we do not Sabbath because of fear. Fear that we won't get it all done. Fear that we will not have enough money. Fear that we have to work more. This fear is driven by an impoverished spirit. It is the spirit of poverty. A person could have one billion dollars but still have the spirit of poverty. Or a person could have two dollars and have the spirit of poverty. It is not related to how much money we have. The impoverished spirit is directly tied to a lack of faith in the sovereignty of the Lord's provision in our lives. When we have an impoverished spirit, it is dangerous because it makes us believe that we are lacking. We will use anything to fill up the emptiness in us: food, pornography, alcohol, or substance abuse. We feel that we are lacking, so we take our anger out on those we love so we can feel better about ourselves.

All of these things are because of an impoverished spirit. FOMO—fear of missing out. We fear we are missing something. But the Lord says that if we rest with Him, He will fill us up and kill the spirit of fear. He does it through something called trust.

Have you ever heard of a trust fall? We use them in team building. They are actually very successful! If you do not know what a trust fall is, it is when someone goes to a ledge and falls backward, on purpose, trusting the people below to safely catch him or her. There is a bond that is built between the person who falls and the people that catch them that later has an effect when they need that faith and trust in one another. It is a practice to build trust.

Here is what trust does. Trust builds faith and faith dispels fear. The enemy wants to bring fear upon us, but when we sit down for the Sabbath, we are showing the enemy that instead of fear, we choose faith in God. We are saying, "God, I trust You." And God fills us with faith, and immediately the fear begins to flee. We do not need to earn more on the Sabbath. We rest as if all the work is done and trust that the Lord is God.

God has already done all the work. We can rest because the work is done. And as believers in Christ, we can truly live in a place of knowing that the work is actually done. In John 19:30, it says, *"When He had received the drink, Jesus said, 'It is finished.' With that, He bowed His head and gave up His spirit."* All the work that was necessary was finished on the cross of Christ. The work that destroyed sin and death was finished on the cross of Christ. The work that gives us an identity as a son or a daughter of the King was finished on the cross of Christ. The work that gives us a profound purpose, a reason for living, was finished on the cross of Christ. The work that ensures eternal peace over our souls was finished on the cross of Christ. He finished all the work that is necessary for identity, purpose, peace, and salvation. Nothing we do will give us more than what we already have in Christ. You plus Jesus equals Jesus. He has already done it all. The finished work of Jesus leads us to rest.

What is the Holy Spirit asking you to do? Are you willing to step out in faith and do what God is asking you to do? Do you trust God enough to rest the way He wants you to rest?

Psalm 23:6 says that the goodness and mercy of God is following after you every day of your life. He has been running behind you all your life trying to get you to rest in Him. He is chasing you with goodness. He wants to be the foundation of your life. He loves you and wants to give you power and strength and fulfillment through the rest that only He can provide.

SEVENTEEN

THE PAST FIVE YEARS

ANXIETY STARTED THIS story. Sabbath ended it. Through the faithful practice of the Sabbath, God returned to me something that I thought was gone forever. Peace. Shalom. Everything as it should be. During the worst of my bout with anxiety, I had a lie creep into me that maybe many of us have felt. "This is never going to go away." For me, I remember distinctly standing in the shower and weeping over my new reality. I was going to struggle with anxiety for the rest of my life. Not only that, but considering the progression of my life from no anxiety to now crushing anxiety, the evidence pointed that each day, as bad as it was, was going to be better than the days that lay ahead. Not only was my anxiety not going away, but it was also going to get worse and worse.

A counselor I saw for roughly a year told me to treat my episodes of anxiety as a passing moment, not a lifestyle. In fact, he shared with me that when fear creeps in, don't let the boat come into the harbor. Let it pass by. Recognize it, but don't digest it. Let it sail away on the river. But crazy ol' me just thought, "What if this is a lazy river that just continues in a circle? This boat will be back here in about 12 minutes." The counselor then suggested, "OK, see the fear tied to a helium balloon floating away from you. Don't grab the string; let that balloon go." Still not convinced, I retorted, "Until a bird pops the balloon and its contents fall on my head once again."

The point I was making with the counselor was that I don't just want to pretend like this anxiety doesn't exist—plug my ears and duck my head in the sand. Rather, I want to deal with the fear. Remedy it. For good. While the counseling was helpful in stewarding the feelings of fear, it was not dealing with the reason for the fear. I don't want to put the mean, violent dog on a leash. I want to take it out back and send it to Jesus.

My problem that led to panic and anxiety, as mentioned before, was accumulated stress. I had no remedy for the stress—that is, until Sabbath entered my life. The practice of 24 hours with the Lord reset my equilibrium of peace. Sabbath recalibrated my heart around what matters most. And of greatest importance, Sabbath connected me to the Father like never before. The wellspring of life-giving deposits from His vast wealth of strength was all I needed. What I was facing and continue to face in this life I could not handle. But my Father could, and did, and will.

In the last five years our family has spent many Friday nights gathered around our table. The stole goes around my neck, the candles are lit, the bread wafts its delicious reminder of God's goodness. After the meal, the blessings are shared one by one. As a fantastic addition, many, many people have joined us around the table and participated in the Shabbat meal with us. Friends of our kids who are staying over for the night. Families going through trials. People we love to share life with and thus want to share the most important part of our lives with. In fact, our family of five is not incredibly great at traditions as some families are. I've wondered at times throughout the nearly 23 years we've had kids, what will our kids take from us and pass down to their families? A love of God? Certainly. Fandom of the Florida Gators? Hopefully! But what about traditions that remind them of more than an activity repeated? Christine and I have incredible peace believing that of all the things they might include in their one-day families' traditions, the Shabbat meal and practice of the Sabbath will be one. It's a legacy of faith, rest, and peace. Sounds delightful because it is delightful.

Interestingly enough, I am a forgetful man. As I tell our staff at illuminate church from time to time, "Vision leaks." We must be C.R.O.'s. Chief Reminding Officers. As the pace of life and the flurry of needs surround us, we often forget what it is that keeps us as people rooted to the love of God. We can find that our new level of spiritual growth and maturity in the Lord gives us an air of self-confidence that belies the truth: We feel great because of Jesus, not because of self. We need to remember this. As a family, there are seasons where we will look up and realize that either we are just going through the motions with no meaning (religion can be like that) or we simply skipped a week or four of Sabbath due to calendar crush. We perceptibly notice a change in family dynamics. Similar to a baby that hasn't been fed, slept, or changed, we begin to cry out. Something is amiss. And that something is a lack of healthy Sabbath practice. We can feel it when we miss it. People around me miss me when I don't Sabbath. I get replaced by a more tired, wound-up, irritable version of myself. We must Sabbath.

I invite you to do the same. Sabbath. You may not have known you were in sin by not Sabbathing before picking up this book, but now you know the truth, and the truth can set you free—yes, *will* set you free if you live it. Learn to rest God's way. You'll thank Him for it.

ABOUT THE AUTHOR

Tim Ingram is the founding and lead pastor of illuminate church, a vibrant faith community just outside the house of Mickey Mouse in Kissimmee, FL.

A military brat, Tim grew up in far flung places such as Alaska and Germany but has called Florida home since 1987.

A graduate of the University of Florida and Asbury Theological Seminary, Tim's main passion is to help people find abundant life in Jesus.

He and his wife, Christine, have three children although two are now adults.

They reside in Celebration , FL.

Made in the USA
Monee, IL
17 May 2025

17564868R00089